THE PART PLAYED BY INFANCY IN THE EVOLUTION OF MAN

JOHN FISKE

[John Fiske attained distinction in three distinct fields of letters: as a historian, as a scientific interpreter of religion, as an expositor of the philosophy of evolution. In this last department of his work his original contribution was the theory here set forth, taken from a chapter in "A Century of Science and Other Essays," copyright by Houghton, Mifflin & Co., Boston and New York, 1900. Mr. Fiske died in 1901, in his sixtieth year.]

When Darwin's "Origin of Species" was first published, when it gave us that wonderful explanation of the origin of forms of life from allied forms through the operation of natural selection, it must have been like a mental illumination to every person who comprehended it. But after all it left a great many questions unexplained, as was natural. It accounted for the phenomena of organic development in general with wonderful success, but it must have left a great many minds with the feeling: If man has been produced in this way, if the mere operation of natural selection has produced the human race, wherein is the human race anyway essentially different from lower races? Is not man really dethroned, taken down from that exceptional position in which we have been accustomed to place him, and might it not be possible, in the course of the future, for other beings to come upon the earth as far superior to man as man is superior to the fossilized dragons of Jurassic antiquity?

Such questions used to be asked, and when they were asked, although one might have a very strong feeling that it was not so, at the same time one could not exactly say why. One could not then find any scientific argument for objections to that point of view. But with the further development of the question the whole subject began gradually to wear a different appearance; and I am going to give you a little bit of autobiography, because I think it may be of some interest in this connection. I am going to mention two or three of the successive stages which the whole question took in my own mind as one thing came up after another, and how from time to time it began to dawn upon me that I had up to that point been looking at the problem from not exactly the right point of view.

When Darwin's "Descent of Man" was published in 1871, it was of course a book characterized by all his immense learning, his wonderful fairness of spirit and fertility of suggestion. Still, one could not but feel that it did not solve the question of the origin of man. There was one great contrast between that book and his "Origin of Species." In the earlier treatise he undertook to point out a *vera causa* [true cause] of the origin of species, and he did it. In his "Descent of Man" he brought together a great many minor generalizations which facilitated the understanding of man's origin. But he did not come at all near to solving the central problem, nor did he anywhere show clearly why the natural selection might not have gone on forever producing one set of beings after another distinguishable chiefly by physical differences. But Darwin's co-discoverer, Alfred Russel Wallace, at an early stage in his researches, struck out a most brilliant and pregnant suggestion. In that one respect Wallace went further than ever Darwin did. It was a point of which, indeed, Darwin admitted the importance. It was a point of which nobody could fail to understand the importance, that in the course of the evolution of a very highly organized animal, if there came a point at which it was of more advantage to that animal to have variations in his intelligence seized upon and improved by natural selection than to have physical changes seized upon, then natural selection would begin working almost exclusively upon that creature's intelligence, and he would develop in intelligence to a great extent, while his physical organism would change but slightly. Now, that of course applied to the case of man, who is changed physically but very slightly from the apes, while he has traversed intellectually such a stupendous chasm.

As soon as this statement was made by Wallace, it seemed to me to open up an entirely new world of speculation. There was this enormous antiquity of man, during the greater part of which he did not know enough to make history. We see man existing here on the earth, no one can say how long, but surely many hundreds of thousands of years, yet only during just the last little fringe of four or five thousand years has he arrived at the point where he makes history. Before that, something was going on, a great many things were going on, while his ancestors were slowly growing up to that point of intelligence where it began to make itself felt in the recording of events. This agrees with Wallace's suggestion of a long period of psychical change, accompanied by slight physical change.

Well, in the spring of 1871, when Darwin's "Descent of Man" came out, just about the same time I happened to be reading Wallace's account of his experiences in the Malay Archipelago, and how at one time he caught a female orang-outang with a new-born baby, and the mother died, and Wallace brought up the baby orang-outang by hand; and this baby orang-outang had a kind of infancy which was a great deal longer than that of a cow or a sheep, but it was nothing compared to human infancy in length. This little orang-outang could not get up and march around, as mammals of less intelligence do, when he was first born, or within three or four days; but after three or four weeks or so he would get up, and begin taking hold of something and pushing it around, just as children push a chair; and he went through a period of staring at his hands, as human babies do, and altogether was a good deal slower in getting to the point where he could take care of himself. And while I was reading of that I thought, Dear me! if there is any one thing in which the human race is signally distinguished from other mammals, it is in the enormous duration of their infancy; but it is a point that I do not recollect ever seeing any naturalist so much as allude to.

It happened at just that time that I was making researches in psychology about the organization of experiences, the way in which conscious intelligent action can pass down into quasi-automatic action, the generation of instincts, and various allied questions; and I thought, Can it be that the increase of intelligence in an animal, if carried beyond a certain point, must necessarily result in prolongation of the period of infancy,—must necessarily result in the birth of the mammal at a less developed stage, leaving something to be done, leaving a good deal to be done, after birth? And then the argument seemed to come along very naturally, that for every action of life, every adjustment which a creature makes in life, whether a muscular adjustment or an intelligent adjustment, there has got to be some registration effected in the nervous system, some line of transit worn for nervous force to follow; there has got to be a connection between certain nerve-centres before the thing can be done, whether it is the acts of the viscera or the acts of the limbs, or anything of that sort; and of course it is obvious that if the creature has not many things to register in his nervous system, if he has a life which is very simple, consisting of few actions that are performed with great frequency, that animal becomes almost automatic in his whole life; and all the nervous connections that need to be made to enable him to carry on life get made during the fœtal period [the period before birth] or during the egg period, and when he comes to be born, he comes all ready to go to work. As one result of this, he does not learn from individual experience, but one generation is like the preceding generations, with here and there some slight modifications. But when you get the creature that has arrived at the point where his experience has become varied, he has got to do a good many things, and there is more or less individuality about them; and many of them are not performed with the same minuteness and regularity, so that there does not begin to be that automatism within the period during which he is being developed and his form is taking on its outlines. During prenatal life [before birth] there is not time enough for all these nervous registrations, and so by degrees it comes about that he is born with his nervous system perfectly capable only of making him breathe and digest food,—of making him do the things absolutely requisite for supporting life; instead of being born with a certain number of definite developed capacities, he has a number of potentialities which have got to be roused according to his own individual experience. Pursuing that line of thought, it began after a while to seem clear to me that the infancy of the animal in a very undeveloped condition, with the larger part of his faculties in potentiality rather than in actuality, was a direct result of the increase of intelligence, and I began to see that now we have two steps: first, natural selection goes on increasing the intelligence; and secondly, when the intelligence goes far enough, it makes a longer infancy, a creature is born less developed, and therefore there comes this plastic period during which he is more teachable. The capacity for progress begins to come in, and you begin to get at one of the great points in which man is distinguished from the lower animals, for one of those points is undoubtedly his progressiveness; and I think that any one will say, with very little hesitation, that if it were not for our period of infancy we should not be progressive. If we came into the world with our capacities all cut and dried, one generation would be very much like another.

Then, looking around to see what are the other points which are most important in which man differs from the lower animals, there comes that matter of the family. The family has adumbrations and foreshadowings among the lower animals, but in general it may be said that while mammals lower than man are gregarious, in man have become established those peculiar relationships which constitute what we know as the family; and it is easy to see how the existence of helpless infants would bring about just that state of things. The necessity of caring for the infants would prolong the period of maternal affection, and would tend to keep the father and mother and children together, but it would tend especially to keep the mother and children together. This business of the marital relations was not really a thing that became adjusted in the primitive ages of man, but it has become adjusted in the course of civilization. Real monogamy, real faithfulness of the male parent, belongs to a comparatively advanced stage; but in the earlier stages the knitting together of permanent relations between mother and infant, and the approximation toward steady relations on the part of the male parent, came to bring about the family and gradually to knit those organizations which we know as clans.

Here we come to another stage, another step forward. The instant society becomes organized in clans, natural selection cannot let these clans be broken up and die out,—the clan becomes the chief object or care of natural selection, because, if you destroy it you retrograde again, you lose all you have gained; consequently, those clans in which the primeval selfish instincts were so modified that the individual conduct would be subordinated to some extent to the needs to the clan,—those are the ones which would prevail in the struggle for life. In this way you gradually get an external standard to which man has to conform his conduct, and you get the germs of altruism and morality; and in the prolonged affectionate relation between the mother and the infant you get the opportunity for that development of altruistic feeling which, once started in those relations, comes into play in the more general relations, and makes more feasible and more workable the bonds which keep society together, and enable it to unite on wider and wider terms.

So it seems that from a very small beginning we are reaching a very considerable result. I had got these facts pretty clearly worked out, and carried them around with me some years, before a fresh conclusion came over me one day with a feeling of surprise. In the old days before the Copernican astronomy was promulgated, man regarded himself as the centre of the universe. He used to entertain theological systems which conformed to his limited knowledge of nature. The universe seemed to be made for his uses, the earth seemed to have been fitted up for his dwelling-place, he occupied the centre of creation, the sun was made to give him light, etc. When Copernicus overthrew that view, the effect upon theology was certainly tremendous. I do not believe that justice has ever been done to the shock that it gave to man when he was made to realize that he occupied a kind of miserable little clod of dirt in the universe, and that there were so many other worlds greater than this. It was one of the first great shocks involved in the change from ancient to modern scientific views, and I do not doubt it was responsible for a great deal of the pessimistic philosophizing that came in the seventeenth and eighteenth centuries.

Now, it flashed upon me a dozen years or so ago—after thinking about this manner in which man originated—that man occupies certainly just as exceptional a position as before, if he is the terminal in a long series of evolutionary events. If at the end of the long history of evolution comes man, if this whole secular process has been going on to produce this supreme object, it does not much matter what kind of a cosmical body he lives on. He is put back into the old position of theological importance, and in a much more intelligent way than in the old days when he was supposed to occupy the centre of the universe. We are enabled to say that while there is no doubt of the evolutionary process going on through countless ages which we know nothing about, yet in the one case where it is brought home to us we spell out an intelligible story, and we do find things working along up to man as a terminal fact in the whole process. This is indeed a consistent conclusion from Wallace's suggestion that natural selection, in working toward the genesis of man, began to follow a new path and make psychical changes instead of physical changes. Obviously, here you are started upon a new chapter in the history of the universe. It is no longer going to be necessary to shape new limbs, and to thicken the skin and make new growths of hair, when man has learned how to build a fire, when he can take some other animal's hide and make it into clothes. You have got to a new state of things.

After I had put together all these additional circumstances with regard to the origination of human society and the development of altruism, I began to see a little further into the matter. It then began to appear that not only is man the terminal factor in a long process of evolution, but in the origination of man there began the development of the higher psychical attributes, and those attributes are coming to play a greater and greater part in the development of the human race. Just take this mere matter of "altruism," as we call it. It is not a pretty word, but must serve for want of a better. In the development of altruism from the low point, where there was scarcely enough to hold the clan together, up to the point reached at the present day, there has been a notable progress, but there is still room for an enormous amount of improvement. The progress has been all in the direction of bringing out what we call the higher spiritual attributes. The feeling was now more strongly impressed upon me than ever, that all these things tended to set the whole doctrine of evolution into harmony with religion; that if the past through which man had originated was such as has been described, then religion was a fit and worthy occupation for man, and some of the assumptions which underlie every system of religion must be true. For example, with regard to the assumption that what we see of the present life is not the whole thing; that there is a spiritual side of the question beside the material side; that, in short, there is for man a life eternal. When I wrote the "Destiny of Man," all that I ventured to say was, that it did not seem quite compatible with ordinary common sense to suppose that so much pains would have been taken to produce a merely ephemeral result. But since then another argument has occurred to me: that just at the time when the human race was beginning to come upon the scene, when the germs of morality were coming in with the family, when society was taking its first start, there came into the human mind—how one can hardly say, but there did come—the beginnings of a groping after something that lies outside and beyond the world of sense. That groping after a spiritual world has been going on here for much more than a hundred thousand years, and it has played an enormous part in the history of mankind, in the whole development of human society. Nobody can imagine what mankind would have been without it up to the present time. Either all religion has been a reaching out for a phantom that does not exist, or a reaching out after something that does exist, but of which man, with his limited intelligence, has only been able to gain a crude idea. And the latter seems a far more probable conclusion, because, if it is not so, it constitutes a unique exception to all the operations of evolution we know about. As a general thing in the whole history of evolution, when you see any internal adjustment reaching out toward something, it is in order to adapt itself to something that really exists; and if the religious cravings of man constitute an exception, they are the one thing in the whole process of evolution that is exceptional and different from all the rest. And this is surely an argument of stupendous and resistless weight.

I take this autobiographical way of referring to these things, in the order in which they came before my mind, for the sake of illustration. The net result of the whole is to put evolution in harmony with religious thought,— not necessarily in harmony with particular religious dogmas or theories, but in harmony with the great religious drift, so that the antagonism which used to appear to exist between religion and science is likely to disappear. So I think it will before a great while. If you take the case of some evolutionist like Professor Haeckel, who is perfectly sure that materialism accounts for everything (he has got it all cut and dried and settled; he knows all about it, so that there is really no need of discussing the subject!); if you ask the question whether it was his scientific study of evolution that really led him to such a dogmatic conclusion, or whether it was that he started from some purely arbitrary assumption, like the French materialists of the eighteenth century, I have no doubt that the latter would be the true explanation. There are a good many people who start on their theories of evolution with these ultimate questions all settled to begin with. It was the most natural thing in the world that after the first assaults of science upon old beliefs, after a certain number of Bible stories and a certain number of church doctrines had been discredited, there should be a school of men who in sheer weariness should settle down to scientific researches, and say, "We content ourselves with what we can prove by the methods of physical science, and we will throw everything else overboard." That was very much the state of mind of the famous French atheists of the last century. But only think how chaotic nature was to their minds compared to what she is to our minds to-day. Just think how we have in the present century arrived where we can see the bearings of one set of facts in nature as collated with another set of facts, and contrast it with the view which even the greatest of those scientific French materialists could take. Consider how fragmentary and how lacking in arrangement was the universe they saw compared with the universe we see to-day, and it is not strange that to them it could be an atheistic world. That hostility between science and religion continued as long as religion was linked hand in hand with the ancient doctrine of special creation. But now that the religious world has unmoored itself, now that it is beginning to see the truth and beauty of natural science and to look with friendship upon conceptions of evolution, I suspect that this temporary antagonism, which we have fallen into a careless way of regarding as an everlasting antagonism, will come to an end perhaps quicker than we realize.

There is one point that is of great interest in this connection, although I can only hint at it. Among the things that happened in that dim past when man was coming into existence was the increase of his powers of manipulation; and that was a factor of immense importance. Anaxagoras, it is said, wrote a treatise in which he maintained that the human race would never have become human if it had not been for the hand. I do not know that there was so very much exaggeration about that. It was certainly of great significance that the particular race of mammals whose intelligence increased far enough to make it worth while for natural selection to work upon intelligence alone was the race which had developed hands and could manipulate things. It was a wonderful era in the history of creation when that creature could take a club and use it for a hammer, or could pry up a stone with a stake, thus adding one more lever to the levers that made up his arm. From that day to this, the career of man has been that of a person who has operated upon his environment in a different way from any animal before him. An era of similar importance came probably somewhat later, when man learned how to build a fire and cook his food. Here was another means of acting upon the environment. Here was the beginning of the working of endless physical and chemical changes through the application of heat, just as the first use of the club or the crowbar was the beginning of an enormous development in the mechanical arts.

Now, at the same time, to go back once more into that dim past, when ethics and religion, manual art and scientific thought, found expression in the crudest form of myths, the æsthetic sense was germinating likewise. Away back in the glacial period you find pictures drawn and scratched upon the reindeer's antler, portraitures of mammoths and primitive pictures of the chase; you see the trinkets, the personal decorations, proving beyond question that the æsthetic sense was there. There has been an immense æsthetic development since then. And I believe that in the future it is going to mean far more to us than we have yet begun to realize. I refer to the kind of training that comes to mankind through direct operation upon his environment, the incarnation of his thought, the putting of his ideas into new material relations. This is going to exert powerful effects of a civilizing kind. There is something strongly educational and disciplinary in the mere dealing with matter, whether it be in the manual training-school, whether it be in carpentry, in overcoming the inherent and total depravity of inanimate things, shaping them to your will, and also in learning to subject yourself to their will (for sometimes you must do that in order to achieve your conquests; in other words, you must humour their habits and proclivities). In all this there is a priceless discipline, moral as well as mental, let alone the fact that, in whatever kind of artistic work a man does, he is doing that which in the very working has in it an element of something outside of egoism; even if he is doing it for motives not very altruistic, he is working toward a result the end of which is the gratification or the benefit of other persons than himself; he is working toward some result which in a measure depends upon their approval, and to that extent tends to bring him into closer relations to his fellow man.

In the future, to an even greater extent than in the recent past, crude labour will be replaced by mechanical contrivances. The kind of labour which can command its price is the kind which has trained intelligence behind it. One of the great needs of our time is the multiplication of skilled and special labour. The demand for the products of intelligence is far greater than that for mere crude products of labour, and it will be more and more so. For there comes a time when the latter products have satisfied the limit to which a man can consume food and drink and shelter,—those things which merely keep the animal alive. But to those things which minister to the requirements of the spiritual side of a man there is almost no limit. The demand one can conceive is well-nigh infinite. One of the philosophical things that have been said, in discriminating man from the lower animals, is that he is the one creature who is never satisfied. It is well for him that he is so, that there is always something more for which he craves. To my mind this fact most strongly hints that man is infinitely more than a mere animate machine.

THE NEW STUDY OF CHILDREN

Top

Professor James Sully

[This eminent writer is Grote Professor of the Philosophy of Mind and of Logic at University College, London. His works published by D. Appleton & Co., New York, are "Illusions," "Outlines of Psychology with Special Reference to the Theory of Education," "Teachers' Handbook of Psychology," "The Human Mind," "Pessimism," "Children's Ways," and "Studies of Childhood." From the last mentioned work, copyright by D. Appleton&Co.,thefollowingistheintr oductorychapter.]

Man has always had the child with him, and one might be sure that since he became gentle and alive to the beauty of things he must have come under the spell of the baby. We have evidence beyond the oft-quoted departure of Hector and other pictures of childish grace in early literature that baby-worship and baby-subjection are not wholly things of modern times. There is a pretty story taken down by Mr. Leland from the lips of an old Indian woman, which relates how Glooskap, the hero-god, after conquering all his enemies, rashly tried his hand at managing a certain baby, Wasis by name, and how he got punished for his rashness.

Yet there is good reason to suppose that it is only within comparatively recent times that the more subtle charm and the deeper significance of infancy have been discerned. We have come to appreciate babyhood as we have come to appreciate the finer lineaments of nature as a whole. This applies of course more especially to the ruder sex. The man has in him much of the boy's contempt for small things, and he needed ages of education at the hands of the better-informed woman before he could perceive the charm of infantile ways.

One of the first males to do justice to this attractive subject was Rousseau. He made short work with the theological dogma that the child is born morally depraved, and can only be made good by miraculous appliances. His watchword, return to nature, included a reversion to the infant as coming virginal and unspoilt by man's tinkering from the hands of its Maker. To gain a glimpse of this primordial beauty before it was marred by man's awkward touch was something, and so Rousseau set men in the way of sitting reverently at the feet of infancy, watching and learning.

For us of to-day, who have learned to go to the pure springs of nature for much of our spiritual refreshment, the child has acquired a high place among the things of beauty. Indeed, the grace of childhood may almost be said to have been discovered by the modern poet. Wordsworth has stooped over his cradle intent on catching, ere they passed, the "visionary gleams" of "the glories he hath known." Blake, R. L. Stevenson, and others, have tried to put into language his day-dreamings, his quaint fancyings. Dickens and Victor Hugo have shown us something of his delicate quivering heart-strings; Swinburne has summed up the divine charm of "children's ways and wiles." The page of modern literature is, indeed, a monument of our child-love and our child-admiration.

Nor is it merely as to a pure untarnished nature that we go back admiringly to childhood. The æsthetic charm of the infant which draws us so potently to its side and compels us to watch its words and actions is, like everything else which moves the modern mind, highly complex. Among other sources of this charm we may discern the perfect serenity, the happy "insouciance" [unconcern] of the childish mind. The note of world-complaint in modern life has penetrated into most domains, yet it has not, one would hope, penetrated into the charmed circle of childish experience. Childhood has, no doubt, its sad aspect:

> Poor stumbler on the rocky coast of woe,
> Tutored by pain each source of pain to know:

neglect and cruelty may bring much misery into the first bright years. Yet the very instinct of childhood to be glad in its self-created world, an instinct which with consummate art Victor Hugo keeps warm and quick in the breast of the half-starved ill-used child Cosette, secures for it a peculiar blessedness. The true nature-child, who has not become used-up, is happy, untroubled with the future, knowing nothing of the misery of disillusion. As, with hearts chastened by many experiences, we take a peep over the wall of his fancy-built pleasance, we seem to be taken back to a real golden age. With Amiel, we say: "The little of paradise which still remains on earth is due to his presence." Yet the thought, which the same moment brings, of the flitting of the nursery visions, of the coming storm and stress, adds a pathos to the spectacle, and we feel as Heine felt when he wrote:

> I look at you and sadness
> Steals into my heart.

Other and strangely unlike feelings mingle with this caressing, half-pitiful admiration. We moderns are given to relieving the strained attitude of reverence and pity by momentary outbursts of humorous merriment. The child, while appealing to our admiration and our pity, makes a large and many-voiced appeal also to our sense of the laughter in things. It is indeed hard to say whether he is most amusing when setting at naught in his quiet, lordly way, our most extolled views, our ideas of what is true and false, of the proper uses of things, and so forth, or when labouring in his perfectly self-conceived fashion to overtake us and be as experienced and as conventional as ourselves. This ever new play of droll feature in childish thought and action forms one of the deepest sources of delight for the modern lover of childhood.

With the growth of a poetic or sentimental interest in childhood there has come a new and different kind of interest. Ours is a scientific age, and science has cast its inquisitive eye on the infant. We want to know what happens in these first all-decisive two or three years of human life, by what steps exactly the wee amorphous thing takes shape and bulk, both physically and mentally. And we can now speak of the beginning of a careful and methodical investigation of child-nature, by men trained in scientific observation. This line of inquiry, started by physicians, as the German Sigismund, in connection with their special professional aims, has been carried on by a number of fathers and others having access to the infant, among whom it may be enough to name Darwin and Preyer.

This eagerness to know what the child is like, an eagerness illustrated further by the number of reminiscences of early years recently published, is the outcome of a many-sided interest which it may be worth while to analyze.

The most obvious source of interest in the doings of infancy lies in its primitiveness. At the cradle we are watching the beginnings of things, the first tentative thrustings forward into life. Our modern science is before all things historical and genetic, going back to beginnings so as to understand the later and more complex phases of things as the outcome of these beginnings. The same kind of curiosity which prompts the geologist to get back to the first stages in the building up of the planet, or the biologist to search out the pristine forms of life, is beginning to urge the student of man to discover by a careful study of infancy the way in which human life begins to take its characteristic forms.

The appearance of Darwin's name among those who have deemed the child worthy of study suggests that the subject is closely connected with natural history. However man in his proud maturity may be related to Nature, it is certain that in his humble inception he is immersed in Nature and saturated with her. As we all know, the lowest races of mankind stand in close proximity to the animal world. The same is true of the infants of civilized races. Their life is outward and visible, forming a part of nature's spectacle; reason and will, the noble prerogatives of humanity, are scarce discernible; sense, appetite, instinct, these animal functions seem to sum up the first year of human life.

To the evolutionist, moreover, the infant exhibits a still closer kinship to the natural world. In the successive stages of fœtal development he sees the gradual unfolding of human lineaments out of a widely typical animal form. And even after birth he can discern new evidences of this genealogical relation of the "lord" of creation to his inferiors. How significant, for example, is the fact recently established by a medical man, Dr. Louis Robinson, that the new-born infant is able just like the ape to suspend his whole weight by grasping a small horizontal rod.

Yet even as nature-object for the biologist the child presents distinctive attributes. Though sharing in animal instinct, he shares in it only to a very small extent. The most striking characteristic of the new-born offspring of man is its unpreparedness for life. Compare with the young of other animals the infant so feeble and incapable. He can neither use his limbs nor see the distance of objects as a new-born chick or calf is able to do. His brain-centres are, we are told, in a pitiable state of undevelopment—and are not even securely encased within their bony covering. Indeed, he resembles for all the world a public building which has to be opened by a given date, and is found when the day arrives to be in a humiliating state of incompleteness.

This fact of the special helplessness of the human offspring at birth, of its long period of dependence on parental or other aids—a period which, probably, tends to grow longer as civilization advances—is rich in biological and sociological significance. For one thing, it presupposes a specially high development of the protective and fostering instincts in the human parents, and particularly the mother—for if the helpless wee thing were not met by these instincts, what would become of our race? It is probable, too, as Mr. Spencer and others have argued, that the institution by nature of this condition of infantile weakness has reacted on the social affections of the race, helping to develop our pitifulness for all frail and helpless things.

Nor is this all. The existence of the infant, with its large and imperative claims, has been a fact of capital importance in the development of social customs. Ethnological researches show that communities have been much exercised with the problem of infancy, have paid it the homage due to its supreme sacredness, girding it about with a whole group of protective and beneficial customs.

Enough has been said, perhaps, to show the far-reaching significance of babyhood to the modern savant. It is hardly too much to say that it has become one of the most eloquent of nature's phenomena, telling us at once of our affinity to the animal world, and of the forces by which our race has, little by little, lifted itself to so exalted a position above this world; and so it has happened that not merely to the perennial baby-worshipper, the mother, and not merely to the poet touched with the mystery of far off things, but to the grave man of science the infant has become a centre of lively interest.

Nevertheless, it is not to the mere naturalist that the babe reveals all its significance. Physical organism as it seems to be more than anything else, hardly more than a vegetative thing indeed, it carries with it the germ of a human consciousness, and this consciousness begins to expand and to form itself into a truly human shape from the very beginning. And here a new source of interest presents itself. It is the human psychologist, the student of those impalpable, unseizable, evanescent phenomena which we call "state of consciousness," who has a supreme interest, and a scientific property in these first years of a human existence. What is of most account in these crude tentatives at living after the human fashion is the play of mind, the first spontaneous manifestations of recognition, of reasoning expectation, of feelings of sympathy and antipathy, of definite persistent purpose.

Rude, inchoate, vague enough, no doubt, are these first groping movements of a human mind: yet of supreme value to the psychologist just because they are the first. If, reflects the psychologist, he can only get at this baby's consciousness so as to understand what is passing there, he will be in an infinitely better position to find his way through the intricacies of the adult consciousness. It may be, as we shall see by-and-by, that the baby's mind is not so perfectly simple, so absolutely primitive as it at first looks. Yet it is the simplest type of human consciousness to which we can have access. The investigator of this consciousness can never take any known sample of the animal mind as his starting point if for no other reason than this, that while possessing many of the elements of the human mind, it presents these in so unlike, so peculiar a pattern.

In this genetic tracing back of the complexities of man's mental life to their primitive elements in the child's consciousness, questions of peculiar interest will arise. A problem which though having a venerable antiquity is still full of meaning concerns the precise relation of the higher forms of intelligence and of sentiment to the elementary facts of the individual's life-experience. Are we to regard all our ideas, even those of God, as woven by the mind out of its experiences, as Locke thought, or have we certain "innate ideas" from the first? Locke thought he could settle this point by observing children. To-day, when the philosophic emphasis is laid not on the date of appearance of the "innate" intuition, but on its originality and spontaneity, this method of interrogating the child's mind may seem less promising. Yet if of less philosophical importance than was once supposed, it is of great psychological importance. There are certain questions, such as that of how we come to see things at a distance from us, which can be approached most advantageously by a study of infant movements. In like manner I believe the growth of a moral sentiment, of that feeling of reverence for duty to which Kant gave so eloquent an expression, can only be understood by the most painstaking observation of the mental activities of the first years.

There is, however, another, and in a sense a larger, source of psychological interest in studying the processes and development of the infant mind. It was pointed out above that to the evolutional biologist the child exhibits man in his kinship to the lower sentient world. This same evolutional point of view enables the psychologist to connect the unfolding of an infant's mind with something which has gone before, with the mental history of the race. According to this way of looking at infancy the successive phases of its mental life are a brief *resume* of the more important features in the slow upward progress of the species. The periods dominated successively by sense and appetite, by blind wondering and superstitious fancy, and by a calmer observation and a juster reasoning about things, these steps mark the pathway both of the child-mind and of the race-mind.

This being so, the first years of a child, with their imperfect verbal expression, their crude fanciful ideas, their seizures by rage and terror, their absorption in the present moment, acquire a new and antiquarian interest. They mirror for us, in a diminished distorted reflection no doubt, the probable condition of primitive man. As Sir John Lubbock and other anthropologists have told us, the intellectual and moral resemblances between the lowest existing races of mankind and children are numerous and close.

Yet this way of viewing childhood is not merely of antiquarian interest. While a monument of his race, and in a manner a key to its history, the child is also its product. In spite of the fashionable Weismannism of the hour, there are evolutionists who hold that in the early manifested tendencies of the child we can discern signs of a hereditary transmission of the effects of ancestral experiences and activities. His first manifestations of rage, for example, are a survival of actions of remote ancestors in their life and death struggles. The impulse of obedience, which is as much a characteristic of the child as that of disobedience, may in like manner be regarded as a transmitted rudiment of a long-practised action of socialized ancestors. This idea of an increment of intelligence and moral disposition, earned for the individual not by himself but by his ancestors, has its peculiar interest. It gives a new meaning to human progress to suppose that the dawn of infant intelligence, instead of being a return to a primitive darkness, contains from the first a faint light reflected on it from the lamp of racial intelligence which has preceded that instead of a return to the race's starting point, the lowest form of the school of experience, it is a start in a higher form, the promotion being a reward conferred on the child for the exertions of his ancestors. Psychological observation will be well employed in scanning the features of the infant's mind in order to see whether they yield evidence of such ancestral dowering.

So much with respect to the rich and varied scientific interest attaching to the movements of the child's mind. It only remains to touch on a third main interest in childhood, the practical or educational interest. The modern world, while erecting the child into an object of æsthetic contemplation, while bringing to bear on him the bull's eye lamp of scientific observation, has become sorely troubled by the momentous problem of rearing him. What was once a matter of instinct and unthinking rule-of-thumb has become the subject of profound and perplexing discussion. Mothers—the right sort of mothers that is—feel that they must know to the core this wee speechless creature which they are called upon to direct into the safe road to manhood. And professional teachers, more particularly the beginners in the work of training, whose work is in some respects the most difficult and the most honourable, have come to see that a clear insight into child-nature and its spontaneous movements must precede any intelligent attempt to work beneficially upon this nature. In this way the teacher has lent his support to the savant and the psychologist in their investigation of infancy. More particularly he has betaken him to the psychologist in order to discover more of the native tendencies and the governing laws of that unformed child-mind which it is his in a special manner to form. In addition to this, the growing educational interest in the spontaneous behaviour of the child's mind may be expected to issue in a demand for a *statistic* of childhood, that is to say, carefully arranged collections of observations bearing on such points as children's questions, their first thoughts about nature, their manifestations of sensibility and insensibility.

The awakening in the modern mind of this keen and varied interest in childhood has led, and is destined to lead still more, to the observation of infantile ways. This observation will, of course, be of very different value according as it subserves the contemplation of the humorous or other æsthetically valuable aspect of child-nature, or as it is directed towards a scientific understanding of this. Pretty anecdotes of children which tickle the emotions may or may not add to our insight into the peculiar mechanism of children's minds. There is no necessary connection between smiling at infantile drolleries and understanding the laws of infantile intelligence. Indeed, the mood of merriment, if too exuberant, will pretty certainly swamp for the moment any desire to understand.

The observation which is to further understanding, which is to be acceptable to science, must itself be scientific. That is to say, it must be at once guided by foreknowledge, specially directed to what is essential in a phenomenon and its surroundings or conditions, and perfectly exact. If anybody supposes this to be easy, he should first try his hand at the work, and then compare what he has seen with what Darwin or Preyer has been able to discover.

How difficult this is may be seen even with reference to the outward physical part of the phenomena to be observed. Ask any mother untrained in observation to note the first appearance of that complex facial movement which we call a smile, and you know what kind of result you are likely to get. The phenomena of a child's mental life, even on its physical and visible side, are of so subtle and fugitive a character that only a fine and quick observation is able to cope with them. But observation of children is never merely seeing. Even the smile has to be interpreted as a smile by a process of imaginative inference. Many careless onlookers would say that a baby smiles in the first days from very happiness, when another and simpler explanation of the movement is forthcoming. Similarly, it wants much fine judgment to say whether an infant is merely stumbling accidentally on an articulate sound, or is imitating your sound. A glance at some of the best memoirs will show how enormously difficult it is to be sure of a right interpretation of these early and comparatively simple manifestations of mind.

Things grow a great deal worse when we try to throw our scientific lasso about the elusive spirit of a child of four or six, and to catch the exact meaning of its swiftly changing movements. Children are, no doubt, at this age frank before the eye of love, and their minds are vastly more accessible than that of the dumb dog that can only look his ardent thoughts. Yet they are by no means so open to view as is often supposed. All kinds of shy reticences hamper them: they feel unskilled in using our cumbrous language; they soon find out that their thoughts are not as ours, but often make us laugh. And how carefully are they wont to hide from our sight their nameless terrors, physical and moral. Much of the deeper childish experience can only reach us, if at all, years after it is over, through the faulty medium of adult memory—faulty even when it is the memory of a Goethe, a George Sand, a Robert Louis Stevenson.

Even when there is perfect candour, and the little one does his best to instruct us as to what is passing in his mind by his "whys" and his "I 'sposes," accompanied by the most eloquent of looks, we find ourselves ever and again unequal to comprehending. Child-thought follows its own paths—roads, as Mr. Rudyard Kipling has well said, "unknown to those who have left childhood behind." The dark sayings of childhood, as when child asks, "Why am I not somebody else?" will be fully illustrated below.

This being so, it might well seem arrogant to speak of any "scientific" investigation of the child's mind; and, to be candid, I may as well confess that, in spite of some recently published highly hopeful forecasts of what child-psychology is going to do for us, I think we are a long way off from a perfectly scientific account of it. Our so-called theories of children's mental activity have so often been hasty generalizations from imperfect observation. Children are probably much more diverse in their ways of thinking and feeling than our theories suppose. But of this more presently. Even where we meet with a common and comparatively prominent trait, we are far as yet from having a perfect comprehension of it. I at least believe that children's play, about which so much has confidently been written, is but imperfectly understood. Is it serious business, half-conscious make-believe, more than half-conscious acting, or, no one of these, or all of them by turns? I think he would be a bold man who ventured to answer this question straight away.

In this state of things it might seem well to wait. Possibly by-and-by we shall light on new methods of tapping the childish consciousness. Patients in a certain stage of the hypnotic trance have returned, it is said, to their childish experience and feelings. Some people do this, or appear to do this, in their dreams. I know a young man who revives vivid recollections of the experiences of the third year of life when he is sleepy, and more especially if he is suffering from a cold. These facts suggest that if we only knew more about the mode of working of the brain we might reinstate a special group of conditions which would secure a re-emergence of childish ideas and sentiments.

Yet our case is not so hopeless that we need defer inquiry into the child's mind until human science has fathomed all the mysteries of the brain. We can know many things of this mind, and these of great importance, even now. The naturalist discusses the actions of the lower animals, confidently attributing intelligent planning here and a germ of vanity or even of moral sense there; and it would be hard were we forbidden to study the little people that are of our own race, and are a thousand times more open to inspection. Really good work has already been done here, and one should be grateful. At the same time, it seems to me of the greatest importance to recognize that it is but a beginning: that the child which the modern world has in the main discovered is after all only half discovered: that if we are to get at his inner life, his playful conceits, his solemn broodings over the mysteries of things, his way of responding to the motley show of life, we must carry this work of noting and interpreting to a much higher point.

Now, if progress is to be made in this work, we must have specially qualified workers. All who know anything of the gross misunderstandings of children of which many so-called intelligent adults are capable, will bear me out when I say that a certain gift of penetration is absolutely indispensable here. If any one asks me what the qualifications of a good child-observer amount to, I may perhaps answer, for the sake of brevity, "A divining faculty, the offspring of child-love, perfected by scientific training." Let us see what this includes.

That the observer of children must be a diviner, a sort of clairvoyant reader of their secret thoughts, seems to me perfectly obvious. Watch half a dozen men who find themselves unexpectedly ushered into a room tenanted by a small child, and you will soon be able to distinguish the diviners, who, just because they have in themselves something akin to the child, seem able at once to get into touch with children. It is probable that women's acknowledged superiority in knowledge of child-nature is owing to their higher gift of sympathetic insight. This faculty, so far from being purely intellectual, is very largely the outgrowth of a peculiar moral nature to which the life of all small things, and of children more than all, is always sweet and congenial. It is very much of a secondary, or acquired instinct; that is, an unreflecting intuition which is the outgrowth of a large experience. For the child-lover seeks the object of his love, and is never so happy as when associating with children and sharing in their thoughts and their pleasures. And it is through such habitual intercourse that there forms itself the instinct or tact by which the significance of childish manifestation is at once unerringly discerned.

There is in this tact or fineness of spiritual touch one constituent so important as to deserve special mention. I mean a lively memory of one's own childhood. As I have observed above, I do not believe in an exact and trustworthy reproduction in later life of particular incidents of childhood. All recalling of past experiences illustrates the modifying influence of the later self in its attempt to assimilate and understand the past self; and this transforming effect is at its maximum when we try to get back to childhood. But though our memory of childhood is not in itself exact enough to furnish facts, it may be sufficiently strong for the purposes of interpreting our observations of the children we see about us. It is said, and said rightly, that in order to read a child's mind we need imagination, and since all imagination is merely readjustment of individual experience, it follows that the skilled decipherer of infantile characters needs before all things to be in touch with his own early feelings and thoughts. And this is just what we find. The vivacious, genial woman who is never so much at home as when surrounded by a bevy of eager-minded children is a woman who remains young in the important sense that she retains much of the freshness and unconventionality of mind, much of the gaiety and expansiveness of early life. Conversely one may feel pretty sure that a woman who retains a vivid memory of her childish ideas and feelings will be drawn to the companionship of children. After reading their autobiographies one hardly needs to be told that Goethe carried into old age his quick responsiveness to the gaiety of the young heart; and that George Sand when grown old was never so happy as when gathering the youngsters about her.

Yet valuable as is this gift of sympathetic insight, it will not, of course, conduce to that methodical, exact kind of observation which is required by science. Hence the need of the second qualification: psychological training. By this is meant that special knowledge which comes from studying the principles of the science, its peculiar problems, and the methods appropriate to these, together with the special skill which is attained by a methodical, practical application of this knowledge in the actual observation and interpretation of manifestations of mind. Thus a woman who wishes to observe to good effect the mind of a child of three must have a sufficient acquaintance with the general course of the mental life to know what to expect, and in what way the phenomena observed have to be interpreted. Really fine and fruitful observation is the outcome of a large knowledge, and anybody who is to carry out in a scientific fashion the observation of the humblest phase of a child's mental life must already know this life as a whole, so far as psychology can as yet describe its characteristics, and determine the conditions of its activity.

And here the question naturally arises: "Who is to carry out this new line of scientific observation?" To begin with the first stage of it, who is to carry out the exact methodical record of the movements of the infant? It is evident that qualification or capacity is not all that is necessary here; capacity must be favoured with opportunity before the work can be actually begun.

It has been pointed out that the pioneers who struck out this new line of experimental research were medical men. The meaning of this fact is pretty apparent. The doctor has not only a turn for scientific observation: he is a privileged person in the nursery. The natural guardians of infancy, the mother and the nurse, exempt him from their general ban on the male. He excepted, no man, not even the child's own father, is allowed to meddle too much with that divine mystery, that meeting point of all the graces and all the beatitudes, the infant.

Consider for a moment the natural prejudice which the inquirer into the characteristics of the infant has to face. Such inquiry is not merely passively watching what spontaneously presents itself; it is emphatically experimenting, that is, the calling out of reactions by applying appropriate stimuli. Even to try whether the new-born babe will close its fingers on your finger when brought into contact with their anterior surface may well seem impious to a properly constituted nurse. To propose to test the wee creature's sense of taste by applying drops of various solutions, as acid, bitters, etc., to the tongue, or to provoke ocular movements to the right or the left, would pretty certainly seem a profanation of the temple of infancy, if not fraught with danger to its tiny deity. And as to trying Dr. Robinson's experiment of getting the newly arrived visitor to suspend his whole precious weight by clasping a bar, it is pretty certain that, women being constituted as at present, only a medical man could have dreamt of so daring a feat.

There is no doubt that baby-worship, the sentimental adoration of infant ways, is highly inimical to the carrying out of a perfectly cool and impartial process of scientific observation. Hence the average mother can hardly be expected to do more than barely to tolerate this encroaching of experiment into the hallowed retreat of the nursery. Even in these days of rapid modification of what used to be thought unalterable sexual characters, one may be bold enough to hazard the prophecy that women who have had scientific training will, if they happen to become mothers, hardly be disposed to give their minds at the very outset to the rather complex and difficult work, say, of making an accurate scientific inventory of the several modes of infantile sensibility, visual, auditory, and so forth, and of the alterations in these from day to day.

It is for the coarser fibred man, then, to undertake much of the earlier experimental work in the investigation of child-nature. And if fathers will duly qualify themselves they will probably find that permission will little by little be given them to carry out investigations, short, of course, of anything that looks distinctly dangerous to the little being's comfort.

At the same time it is evident that a complete series of observations of the infant can hardly be carried out by a man alone. It is for the mother, or some other woman with a pass-key to the nursery, with her frequent and prolonged opportunities of observation to attempt a careful and methodical register of mental progress. Hence the importance of enlisting the mother or her female representative as collaborateur or at least as assistant. Thus supposing the father is bent on ascertaining the exact dates and the order of appearance of the different articulate sounds, which is rather a subject of passive observation than of active experiment; he will be almost compelled to call in the aid of one who has the considerable advantage of passing a good part of each day near the child.[1]

As the wee thing grows and its nervous system becomes more stable and robust more in the way of research may of course be safely attempted. In this higher stage the work of observation will be less simple and involve more of special psychological knowledge. It is a comparatively easy thing to say whether the sudden approach of an object to the eye of a baby a week or so old calls forth the reflex known as blinking: it is a much more difficult thing to say what are the preferences of a child of twelve months in the matter of simple forms, or even colours.

The problem of the order of development of the colour-sense in children looks at first easy enough. Any mother, it may be thought, can say which colours the child first recognizes by naming them when seen, or picking them out when another names them. Yet simple as it looks, the problem is in reality anything but simple. A German investigator, Professor Preyer of Berlin, went to work methodically with his little boy of two years in order to see in what order he would discriminate colours. Two colours, red and green, were first shown, the name added to each, and the child then asked: "Which is red?" "Which is green?" Then other colours were added and the experiments repeated. According to these researches this particular child first acquired a clear discriminative awareness of yellow. Preyer's results have not, however, been confirmed by other investigators, as M. Binet, of Paris, who followed a similar method of inquiry. Thus according to Binet it is not yellow but blue which carries the day in the competition for the child's preferential recognition.

What, it may be asked, is the explanation of this? Is it that children differ in the mode of development of their colour-sensibility to this extent, or can it be that there is some fault in the method of investigation? It has been recently suggested that the mode of testing colour-discrimination by naming is open to the objection that a child may get hold of one verbal sound as "red" more easily than another as "green" and that this would facilitate the recognition of the former. If in this way the recognition of a colour is aided by the retention of its name, we must get rid of this disturbing element of sound. Accordingly new methods of experiment have been attempted in France and America. Thus Professor Baldwin investigates the matter by placing two colours opposite the child's two arms and noting which is reached out to by right or left arm, which is ignored. He has tabulated the results of a short series of these simple experiments for testing childish preference, and supports the conclusions of Binet, as against those of Preyer, that blue comes in for the first place in the child's discriminative recognition.[2] It is, however, easy to see that this method has its own characteristic defects. Thus, to begin with, it evidently does not directly test colour-discrimination at all, but the liking for or interest in colours, which though it undoubtedly implies a measure of discrimination must not be confused with this. And even as a test of preference it is very likely to be misapplied. Thus supposing that the two colours are not equally bright, then the child will grasp at one rather than at the other, because it is a brighter object and not because it is this particular colour. Again if one colour falls more into the first and fresh period of the exercise when the child is fresh and active, whereas another falls more into the second period when he is tired and inactive, the results would, it is evident, give too much value to the former. Similarly, if one colour were brought in after longer intervals of time than another it would have more attractive force through its greater novelty.

Enough has been said to show how very delicate a problem we have here to deal with. And if scientific men are still busy settling the point how the problem can be best dealt with, it seems hopeless for the amateur to dabble in the matter.

I have purposely chosen a problem of peculiar complexity and delicacy in order to illustrate the importance of that training which makes the mental eye of the observer quick to analyse the phenomenon to be dealt with so as to take in all its conditions. Yet there are many parts of this work of observing the child's mind which do not make so heavy a demand on technical ability, but can be done by any intelligent observer prepared for the task by a reasonable amount of psychological study. I refer more particularly to that rich and highly interesting field of exploration which opens up when the child begins to talk. It is in the spontaneous utterances of children, their first quaint uses of words, that we can best watch the play of the instinctive tendencies of thought. Children's talk is always valuable to a psychologist; and for my part I would be glad of as many anecdotal records of their sayings as I could collect.

Here, then, there seems to be room for a relatively simple and unskilled kind of observing work. Yet it would be a mistake to suppose that even this branch of child-observation requires nothing but ordinary intelligence. To begin with, we are all prone, till by special training we have learned to check the inclination, to read far too much of our older thought and sentiment into children. As M. Drox observes, "we are the dupes of ourselves when we observe the babe."

Again, there is a subtle source of error connected with the very attitude of undergoing examination which only a carefully trained observer of childish ways will avoid. A child is very quick in spying whether he is being observed, and as soon as he suspects that you are specially interested in his talk he is apt to try to produce an effect. This wish to say something startling, wonderful, or what not, will, it is obvious, detract from the value of the utterance.

But once more the saying which it is so easy to report has had its history, and the observer who knows something of psychology will look out for facts, that is to say, experiences of the child, suggestions made by others' words which throw light on the saying. No fact is really quite simple, and the reason why some facts look so simple is that the observer does not include in his view all the connections of the occurrence which he is inspecting. The unskilled observer of children is apt to send scraps, fragments of facts, which have not their natural setting. The value of psychological training is that it makes one as jealously mindful of wholeness in facts as a housewife of wholeness in her porcelain. It is, indeed, only when the whole fact is before us, in well-defined contour, that we can begin to deal with its meaning. Thus although those ignorant of psychology may assist us in this region of fact-finding, they can never accomplish that completer and exacter kind of observation which we dignify by the name of Science.

One may conclude then that women may be fitted to become valuable labourers in this new field of investigation, if only they will acquire a genuine scientific interest in babyhood, and a fair amount of scientific training. That a large number of women will get so far is I think doubtful: the sentimental or æsthetic attraction of the baby is apt to be a serious obstacle to a cold matter-of-fact examination of it as a scientific specimen. The natural delight of a mother in every new exhibition of infantile wisdom or prowess is liable to blind her to the exceedingly modest significance of the child's performances as seen from the scientific point of view. Yet as I have hinted, this very fondness for infantile ways, may, if only the scientific caution is added, prove a valuable excitant to study. In England, and in America, there are already a considerable number of women who have undergone some serious training in psychology, and it may not be too much to hope that before long we shall have a band of mothers and aunts busily engaged in noting and recording the movements of children's minds.

I have assumed here that what is wanted is careful studies of individual children as they may be approached in the nursery. And these records of individual children, after the pattern of Preyer's monograph, are I think our greatest need. We are wont to talk rather too glibly about that abstraction, "the child," as if all children rigorously corresponded to one pattern, of which pattern we have a perfect knowledge. Mothers at least know that this is not so. Children of the same family will be found to differ very widely (within the comparatively narrow field of childish traits), as, for example, in respect of matter-of-factness, of fancifulness, of inquisitiveness. Thus, while it is probably true that most children at a certain age are greedy of the pleasures of the imagination, Nature in her well-known dislike of monotony has taken care to make a few decidedly unimaginative. We need to know much more about these variations: and what will best help us here is a number of careful records of infant progress, embracing examples not only of different sexes and temperaments, but also of different social conditions and nationalities. When we have such a collection of monographs we shall be in a much better position to fill out the hazy outline of our abstract conception of childhood with definite and characteristic lineaments.

At the same time I gladly allow that other modes of observation are possible and in their way useful. This applies to older children who pass into the collective existence of the school-class. Here something like collective or statistical inquiry may be begun, as that into the contents of children's minds, their ignorances and misapprehensions about common objects. Some part of this inquiry into the minds of school children may very well be undertaken by an intelligent teacher. Thus it would be valuable to have careful records of children's progress carried out by pre-arranged tests, so as to get collections of examples of mental activity at different ages. More special lines of inquiry having a truly experimental character might be carried out by experts, as those already begun with reference to children's "span of apprehension," *i.e.*, the number of digits or nonsense syllables that can be reproduced after a single hearing, investigations into the effects of fatigue on mental processes, into the effect of number of repetitions on the certainty of reproduction, into musical sensitiveness and so forth.

Valuable as such statistical investigation undoubtedly is, it is no substitute for the careful methodical study of the individual child. This seems to me the greatest desideratum just now. Since the teacher needs for practical reasons to make a careful study of individuals he might well assist here. In these days of literary collaboration it might not be amiss for a kindergarten teacher to write an account of a child's mind in co-operation with the mother. Such a record if well done would be of the greatest value. The co-operation of the mother seems to me quite indispensable, since even where there is out-of-class intercourse between teacher and pupil the knowledge acquired by the former never equals that of the mother.

FOOTNOTES:

[1] The great advantage which the female observer of the infant's mind has over her male competitor is clearly illustrated in some recent studies of childhood by American women. I would especially call attention to a study by Miss M. W. Shinn, (University of California series) *Notes on the Development of a Child* (the writer's niece), where the minute and painstaking record (e.g. of the child's colour-discrimination and visual space exploration) points to the ample opportunity of observation which comes more readily to women.

[2] "Mental Development in the Child and the Race," chap. III.

TWINS, THEIR HISTORY AS A CRITERION OF THE RELATIVE POWERS OF NATURE AND NURTURE

FRANCIS GALTON

[Francis Galton, a cousin of Charles Darwin, has won eminence by bringing problems of human development to the test of statistical inquiry. Among his works are "Hereditary Genius," "English Men of Science, Their Nature and Nurture," "Human Faculty," and "Natural Inheritance." The study of Twins here presented is taken from "Human Faculty," published by Macmillan & Co., London, 1883.]

The exceedingly close resemblance attributed to twins has been the subject of many novels and plays, and most persons have felt a desire to know upon what basis of truth those works of fiction may rest. But twins have many other claims to attention, one of which will be discussed in the present memoir. It is, that their history affords means of distinguishing between the effects of tendencies received at birth, and of those that were imposed by the circumstances of their after lives; in other words, between the effects of nature and of nurture. This is a subject of especial importance in its bearings on investigations into mental heredity, and I, for my part, have keenly felt the difficulty of drawing the necessary distinction whenever I tried to estimate the degree in which mental ability was, on the average, inherited. The objection to statistical evidence in proof of its inheritance has always been: "The persons whom you compare may have lived under similar social conditions and have had similar advantages of education, but such prominent conditions are only a small part of those that determine the future of each man's life. It is to trifling accidental circumstances that the bent of his disposition and his success are mainly due, and these you leave wholly out of account—in fact, they do not admit of being tabulated, and therefore your statistics, however plausible at first sight, are really of very little use." No method of enquiry which I have been able to carry out—and I have tried many methods—is wholly free from this objection. I have therefore attacked the problem from the opposite side, seeking for some new method by which it would be possible to weigh in just scales the respective effects of nature and nurture, and to ascertain their several shares in framing the disposition and intellectual ability of men. The life history of twins supplies what I wanted. We might begin by enquiring about twins who were closely alike in boyhood and youth, and who were educated together for many years, and learn whether they subsequently grew unlike, and, if so, what the main causes were which, in the opinion of the family, produced the dissimilarity. In this way we may obtain much direct evidence of the kind we want; but we can also obtain yet more valuable evidence by a converse method. We can enquire into the history of twins who were exceedingly unlike in childhood, and learn how far they became assimilated under the influence of their identical nurtures; having the same home, the same teachers, the same associates, and in every other respect the same surroundings.

My materials were obtained by sending circulars of enquiry to persons who were either twins themselves or the near relations of twins. The printed questions were in thirteen groups; the last of them asked for the addresses of other twins known to the recipient who might be likely to respond if I wrote to them. This happily led to a continually widening circle of correspondence, which I pursued until enough material was accumulated for a general reconnaissance of the subject.

The reader will easily understand that the word "twins" is a vague expression, which covers two very dissimilar events; the one corresponding to the progeny of animals that have usually more than one young one at a birth, and the other corresponding to those double-yolked eggs that are due to two germinal spots in a single ovum. The consequence of this is, that I find a curious discontinuity in my results. One would have expected that twins would commonly be found to possess a certain average likeness to one another; that a few would greatly exceed that degree of likeness, and a few would greatly fall short of it; but this is not at all the case. Twins may be divided into three groups, so distinct that there are not many intermediate instances; namely, strongly alike, moderately alike, and extremely dissimilar. When the twins are a boy and a girl, they are never closely alike; in fact, their origin never corresponds to that of the above-mentioned double-yolked eggs.

I have received about eighty returns of cases of close similarity, thirty-five of which entered into many instructive details. In a few of these not a single point of difference could be specified. In the remainder, the colour of the hair and eyes were almost always identical; the height, weight, and strength were generally very nearly so, but I have a few cases of a notable difference in these, notwithstanding the resemblance was otherwise very near. The manner and address of the thirty-five pairs of twins is usually described as being very similar, though there often exists a difference of expression familiar to near relatives but unperceived by strangers. The intonation of the voice when speaking is commonly the same, but it frequently happens that the twins sing in different keys. Most singularly, that one point in which similarity is rare is the handwriting. I cannot account for this, considering how strongly handwriting runs in families, but I am sure of the fact. I have only one case in which nobody, not even the twins themselves, could distinguish their own notes of lectures, etc.; barely two or three in which the handwriting was undistinguishable by others, and only a few in which it was described as closely alike. On the other hand, I have many in which it is stated to be unlike, and some in which it is alluded to as the only point of difference.

One of my enquiries was for anecdotes as regards the mistakes made by near relatives between the twins. They are numerous, but not very varied in character. When the twins are children, they have commonly to be distinguished by ribbons tied round their wrist or neck; nevertheless the one is sometimes fed, physicked, and whipped by mistake for the other, and the description of these little domestic catastrophes is usually given to me by the mother, in a phraseology that is somewhat touching by reason of its seriousness. I have one case in which a doubt remains whether the children were not changed in their bath, and the presumed A is not really B, and *vice versa*. In another case an artist was engaged on the portraits of twins who were between three and four years of age; he had to lay aside his work for three weeks, and, on resuming it, could not tell to which child the respective likenesses he had in hand belonged. The mistakes are less numerous on the part of the mother during the boyhood and girlhood of the twins, but almost as frequent on the part of strangers. I have many instances of tutors being unable to distinguish their twin pupils. Thus, two girls used regularly to impose on their music teacher when one of them wanted a whole holiday; they had their lessons at separate hours, and the one girl sacrificed herself to receive two lessons on the same day, while the other one enjoyed herself. Here is a brief and comprehensive account: "Exactly alike in all, their schoolmasters never could tell them apart; at dancing parties they constantly changed partners without discovery; their close resemblance is scarcely diminished by age." The following is a typical schoolboy anecdote: Two twins were fond of playing tricks, and complaints were frequently made; but the boys would never own which was the guilty one, and the complainants were never certain which of the two he was. One head master used to say he would never flog the innocent for the guilty, and another used to flog both. No less than nine anecdotes have reached me of a twin seeing his or her reflection in a looking-glass, and addressing it, in the belief it was the other twin in person. I have many anecdotes of mistakes when the twins were nearly grown up. Thus: "Amusing scenes occurred at college when one twin came to visit the other; the porter on one occasion refused to let the visitor out of the college gates, for, though they stood side by side, he professed ignorance as to which he ought to allow to depart."

Children are usually quick in distinguishing between their parents and his or her twin: but I have two cases to the contrary. Thus, the daughter of a twin says: "Such was the marvellous similarity of their features, voice, manner, etc. that I remember, as a child, being very much puzzled, and I think, had my aunt lived much with us, I should have ended by thinking I had two mothers." The other, a father of twins, remarks: "We were extremely alike, and are so at this moment, so much so that our children up to five and six years old did not know us apart."

I have four or five instances of doubt during an engagement of marriage. Thus: "A married first, but both twins met the lady together for the first time, and fell in love with her there and then. A managed to see her home and to gain her affection, though B went sometimes courting in his place, and neither the lady nor her parents could tell which was which." I have also a German letter, written in quaint terms, about twin brothers who married sisters, but could not easily be distinguished by them. In the well-known novel by Mr. Wilkie Collins of "Poor Miss Finch," the blind girl distinguishes the twin she loves by the touch of his hand, which gives her a thrill that the touch of the other brother does not. Philosophers have not, I believe, as yet investigated the conditions of such thrills; but I have a case in which Miss Finch's test would have failed. Two persons, both friends of a certain twin lady, told me that she had frequently remarked to them that "kissing her twin sister was not like kissing her other sisters, but like kissing herself—her own hand, for example."

It would be an interesting experiment for twins who were closely alike, to try how far dogs could distinguish between them by scent.

I have a few anecdotes of strange mistakes made between twins in adult life. Thus, an officer writes: "On one occasion when I returned from foreign service my father turned to me and said, 'I thought you were in London,' thinking I was my brother—yet he had not seen me for nearly four years—our resemblance was so great."

The next and last anecdote I shall give is, perhaps, the most remarkable of those that I have: it was sent me by the brother of the twins, who were in middle life at the time of its occurrence: "A was again coming home from India, on leave; the ship did not arrive for some days after it was due; the twin brother B had come up from his quarters to receive A, and their old mother was very nervous. One morning A rushed in, saying, 'Oh, mother, how are you?' Her answer was, 'No, B, it's a bad joke; you know how anxious I am!' and it was a little time before A could persuade her that he was the real man."

Enough has been said to prove that an extremely close personal resemblance frequently exists between twins of the same sex; and that, although the resemblance usually diminishes as they grow into manhood and womanhood, some cases occur in which the resemblance is lessened in a hardly perceptible degree. It must be borne in mind that the divergence of development, when it occurs, need not be ascribed to the effect of different nurtures, but that it is quite possible that it may be due to the appearance of qualities inherited at birth, though dormant, like gout, in early life. To this I shall recur.

There is a curious feature in the character of the resemblance between twins, which has been alluded to by a few correspondents: it is well illustrated by the following quotations. A mother of twins says: "There seems to be a sort of interchangeable likeness in expression, that often gave to each the affect of being more like his brother than himself." Again, two twin brothers, writing to me, after analysing their points of resemblance, which are close and numerous, and pointing out certain shades of difference, add: "These seem to have marked us through life, though for a while when we were first separated, the one to go to business, and the other to college, our respective characters were inverted; we both think that at that time we each ran into the character of the other. The proof of this consists in our own recollections, in our correspondence by letter, and in the views which we then took of matters in which we were interested." In explanation of this apparent interchangeableness, we must recollect that no character is simple, and that in twins who strongly resemble each other every expression in the one may be matched by a corresponding expression in the other, but it does not follow that the same expression should be the dominant one in both cases. Now it is by their dominant expressions that we should distinguish between the twins; consequently when one twin has temporarily the expression which is the dominant one in his brother, he is apt to be mistaken for him. There are also cases where the development of the two twins is not strictly by equal steps; they reach the same goal at the same time, but not by identical stages. Thus: A is born the larger, then B overtakes and surpasses A, the end being that the twins become closely alike. This process would aid in giving an interchangeable likeness at certain periods of their growth, and is undoubtedly due to nature more frequently than to nurture.

Among my thirty-five detailed cases of close similarity, there are no less than seven in which both twins suffered from some special ailment or had some exceptional peculiarity. One twin writes that she and her sister "have both the defect of not being able to come down stairs quickly, which, however, was not born with them, but came on at the age of twenty." Another pair of twins have a slight congenital flexure of one of the joints of the little finger: it was inherited from a grandmother, but neither parents, nor brothers, nor sisters show the least trace of it. In another case, one was born ruptured, and the other became so at six months old. Two twins at the age of twenty-three were attacked by toothache, and the same tooth had to be extracted in each case. There are curious and close correspondences mentioned in the falling off of the hair. Two cases are mentioned of death from the same disease; one of which is very affecting. The outline of the story was that the twins were closely alike and singularly attached, and had identical tastes; they both obtained Government clerkships, and kept house together, when one sickened and died of Bright's disease, and the other also sickened of the same disease and died seven months later.

In no less than nine out of the thirty-five cases does it appear that both twins are apt to sicken at the same time. This implies so intimate a constitutional resemblance, that it is proper to give some quotations in evidence. Thus, the father of two twins says: "Their general health is closely alike; whenever one of them has an illness the other invariably has the same within a day or two, and they usually recover in the same order. Such has been the case with whooping cough, chicken-pox, and measles; also with slight bilious attacks, which they have successively. Latterly, they had a feverish attack at the same time." Another parent of twins says: "If anything ails one of them, identical symptoms *nearly always* appear in the other: this has been singularly visible in two instances during the last two months. Thus, when in London, one fell ill with a violent attack of dysentery, and within twenty-four hours the other had precisely the same symptoms."

A medical man writes of twins with whom he is well acquainted: "Whilst I knew them, for a period of two years, there was not the slightest tendency towards a difference in body or mind; external influences seemed powerless to produce any dissimilarity." The mother of two other twins, after describing how they were ill simultaneously up to the age of fifteen, adds, that they shed their first milk teeth within a few hours of each other.

Trousseau has a very remarkable case (in the chapter on Asthma) in his important work, "Clinique Médicale." It was quoted at length in the original French in Mr. Darwin's "Variation Under Domestication," vol. ii. p. 252. The following is a translation:

"I attended twin brothers so extraordinarily alike, that it was impossible for me to tell which was which without seeing them side by side. But their physical likeness extended still deeper for they had, so to speak, a yet more remarkable pathological resemblance. Thus, one of them, whom I saw at the Néothermes at Paris, suffering from rheumatic ophthalmia, said to me, 'At this instant, my brother must be having an ophthalmia like mine;' and, as I had exclaimed against such an assertion, he showed me a few days afterwards a letter just received by him from his brother, who was at that time at Vienna, and who expressed himself in these words: 'I have my ophthalmia; you must be having yours.' However singular this story may appear, the fact is none the less exact: it has not been told to me by others, but I have seen it myself; and I have seen other analogous cases in my practice. These twins were also asthmatic, and asthmatic to a frightful degree. Though born in Marseilles, they never were able to stay in that town, where their business affairs required them to go, without having an attack. Still more strange, it was sufficient for them to get away only as far as Toulon in order to be cured of the attack caught at Marseilles. They travelled continually, and in all countries, on business affairs, and they remarked that certain localities were extremely hurtful to them, and that in others they were free from all asthmatic symptoms."

I do not like to pass over here a most dramatic tale in the *Psychologie Morbide* of Dr. J. Moreau (de Tours), Médecin de l'Hospice de Bicetre. Paris, 1859, p. 172. He speaks "of two twin brothers who had been confined, on account of monomania, at Bicetre.... Physically the two young men are so nearly alike that the one is easily mistaken for the other. Morally, their resemblance is no less complete, and is most remarkable in its details. Thus, their dominant ideas are absolutely the same. They both consider themselves subject to imaginary persecutions; the same enemies have sworn their destruction, and employ the same means to effect it. Both have hallucinations of hearing. They are both of them melancholy and morose; they never address a word to anybody, and will hardly answer the questions that others address to them. They always keep apart and never communicate with one another. An extremely curious fact which has been frequently noted by the superintendents of their section of the hospital, and by myself, is this: From time to time, at very irregular intervals of two, three, and many months, without appreciable cause, and by the purely spontaneous effect of their illness, a very marked change takes place in the condition of the two brothers. Both of them, at the same time, and often on the same day, rouse themselves from their habitual stupor and prostration; they make the same complaints, and they come of their own accord to the physician, with an urgent request to be liberated. I have seen this strange thing occur, even when they were some miles apart, the one being at Bicetre and the other living at Sainte-Anne."

Dr. Moreau ranked as a very considerable medical authority, but I cannot wholly accept this strange story without fuller information. Dr. Moreau writes it in too off-hand a way to carry the conviction that he had investigated the circumstances with the sceptic spirit and scrupulous exactness which so strange a phenomenon would have required. If full and precise notes of the case exist, they certainly ought to be published at length. I sent a copy of this passage to the principal authorities among the physicians to the insane in England, asking if they had ever witnessed any similar case. In reply, I have received three noteworthy instances, but none to be compared in their exact parallelism with that just given. The details of these three cases are painful, and it is not necessary to my general purpose that I should further allude to them.

There is another curious French case of insanity in twins, which was pointed out to me by Professor Paget, described by Dr. Baume in the *Annales Medico-Psychologiques,* 4 série, vol. i., 1863, p. 312, of which the following is an abstract. The original contains a few more details, but it is too long to quote: Francois and Martin, fifty years of age, worked as railroad contractors between Quimper and Châteaulin. Martin had twice had slight attacks of insanity. On January 15, a box in which the twins deposited their savings was robbed. On the night of January 23-4 both Francois (who lodged at Quimper) and Martin (who lived with his wife and children at St. Lorette, two leagues from Quimper) had the same dream at the same hour, three A. M., and both awoke with a violent start, calling out, "I have caught the thief! I have caught the thief! they are doing injury to my brother!" They were both of them extremely agitated, and gave way to similar extravagances, dancing and leaping. Martin sprang on his grandchild, declaring that he was the thief, and would have strangled him if he had not been prevented: he then became steadily worse, complained of violent pains in his head, went out of doors on some excuse, and tried to drown himself in the River Steir, but was forcibly stopped by his son, who had watched and followed him. He was then taken to an asylum by gendarmes, where he died in three days. Francois, on his part calmed down on the morning of the 24th, and employed the day in enquiring about the robbery. By a strange chance he crossed his brother's path at the moment when the latter was struggling with the gendarmes; then he himself became maddened, giving way to extravagant gestures and making incoherent proposals (similar to those of his brother). He then asked to be bled, which was done, and afterwards, declaring himself to be better, went out on the pretext of executing some commission, but really to drown himself in the River Steir, which he actually did, at the very spot where Martin had attempted to do the same thing a few hours previously.

The next point which I shall mention, in illustration of the extremely close resemblance between certain twins, is the similarity in the association of their ideas. No less than eleven out of the thirty-five cases testify to this. They make the same remarks on the same occasion, begin singing the same song at the same moment, and so on; or one would commence a sentence, and the other would finish it. An observant friend graphically described to me the effect produced on her by two such twins whom she had met casually. She said: "Their teeth grew alike, they spoke alike and together, and said the same things, and seemed just like one person." One of the most curious anecdotes that I have received concerning this similarity of ideas was that one twin A, who happened to be at a town in Scotland, bought a set of champagne glasses which caught his attention, as a surprise for his brother B; while at the same time, B, being in England, bought a similar set of precisely the same pattern as a surprise for A. Other anecdotes of a like kind have reached me about these twins.

The last point to which I shall allude regards the tastes and dispositions of the thirty-five pairs of twins. In sixteen cases—that is, in nearly one half of them—these were described as closely similar; in the remaining nineteen they were much alike, but subject to certain named differences. These differences belonged almost wholly to such groups of qualities as these: The one was the more vigorous, fearless, energetic; the other was gentle, clinging, and timid: or, again, the one was more ardent, the other more calm and gentle; or again, the one was the more independent, original, and self-contained; the other the more generous, hasty, and vivacious. In short the difference was always that of intensity or energy in one or other of its protean forms: it did not extend more deeply into the structure of the characters. The more vivacious might be subdued by ill health, until he assumed the character of the other; or the latter might be raised by excellent health to that of the former. The difference is in the key-note, not in the melody.

It follows from what has been said concerning the similar dispositions of the twins, the similarity in the associations of their ideas, of their special ailments, and of their illnesses generally, that the resemblances are not superficial, but extremely intimate. I have only two cases altogether of a strong bodily resemblance being accompanied by mental diversity, and one case only of the converse kind. It must be remembered that the conditions which govern extreme likeness between twins are not the same as those between ordinary brothers and sisters (I may have hereafter to write further about this); and that it would be wholly incorrect to generalize from what has just been said about the twins, that mental and bodily likeness are invariably co-ordinate; such being by no means the case.

We are now in a position to understand that the phrase "close similarity" is no exaggeration, and to realize the value of the evidence about to be adduced. Here are thirty-five cases of twins who were "closely alike" in body and mind when they were young, and who have been reared exactly alike up to their early manhood and womanhood. Since then the conditions of their lives have changed; what change of conditions has produced the most variation?

It was with no little interest that I searched the records of the thirty-five cases for an answer; and they gave an answer that was not altogether direct, but it was very distinct, and not at all what I had expected. They showed me that in some cases the resemblance of body and mind had continued unaltered up to old age, notwithstanding very different conditions of life; and they showed in the other cases that the parents ascribed such dissimilarity as there was wholly, or almost wholly, to some form of illness. In four cases it was scarlet fever; in one case, typhus; in one, a slight effect was ascribed to a nervous fever: then I find effects from an Indian climate; from an illness (unnamed) of nine months' duration; from varicose veins; from a bad fracture of the leg, which prevented all active exercise afterwards; and there were three other cases of ill health. It will be sufficient to quote one of the returns; in this the father writes:

"At birth they were *exactly* alike, except that one was born with a bad varicose affection, the effect of which had been to prevent any violent exercise, such as dancing, or running, and, as she has grown older, to make her more serious and thoughtful. Had it not been for this infirmity, I think the two would have been as exactly alike as it is possible for two women to be, both mentally and physically; even now they are constantly mistaken for one another."

In only a very few cases is there some allusion to the dissimilarity being partly due to the combined action of many small influences, and in no case is it largely, much less wholly, ascribed to that cause. In not a single instance have I met with a word about the growing dissimilarity being due to the action of the firm, free will of one or both of the twins, which had triumphed over natural tendencies; and yet a large proportion of my correspondents happen to be clergymen whose bent of mind is opposed, as I feel assured from the tone of their letters, to a necessitarian view of life.

It has been remarked that a growing diversity between twins may be ascribed to the tardy development of naturally diverse qualities; but we have a right, upon the evidence I have received, to go further than this. We have seen that a few twins retain their close resemblance through life; in other words, instances do exist of thorough similarity of nature, and in these external circumstances do not create dissimilarity. Therefore, in those cases, where there is a growing diversity, and where no external cause can be assigned either by the twins themselves or by their family for it, we may feel sure that it must be chiefly or altogether due to a want of thorough similarity in their nature. Nay further, in some cases it is distinctly affirmed that the growing dissimilarity can be accounted for in no other way. We may therefore broadly conclude that the only circumstance, within the range of those by which persons of similar conditions of life are affected, capable of producing a marked effect on the character of adults, is illness or some accident which causes physical infirmity. The twins who closely resembled each other in childhood and early youth, and were reared under not very dissimilar conditions, either grow unlike through the development of natural characteristics which had lain dormant at first, or else they continue their lives, keeping time like two watches, hardly to be thrown out of accord except by some physical jar. Nature is far stronger than nurture within the limited range that I have been careful to assign to the latter.

The effect of illness, as shown by these replies, is great, and well deserves further consideration. It appears that the constitution of youth is not so elastic as we are apt to think, but that an attack, say of scarlet fever, leaves a permanent mark, easily to be measured by the present method of comparison. This recalls an impression made strongly on my mind several years ago by the sight of a few curves drawn by a mathematical friend. He took monthly measurements of the circumference of his children's heads during the first few years of their lives, and he laid down the successive measurements on the successive lines of a piece of ruled paper, by taking the edge of the paper as a base. He then joined the free ends of the lines, and so obtained a curve of growth. These curves had, on the whole, that regularity of sweep that might have been expected, but each of them showed occasional halts, like the landing places on a long flight of stairs. The development had been arrested by something, and was not made up for by after growth. Now, on the same piece of paper my friend had also registered the various infantile illnesses of the children, and corresponding to each illness was one of these halts. There remained no doubt in my mind that, if these illnesses had been warped off, the development of the children would have been increased by almost the precise amount lost in these halts. In other words, the disease had drawn largely upon the capital, and not only on the income, of their constitutions. I hope these remarks may induce some men of science to repeat similar experiments on their children of the future. They may compress two years of a child's history on one side of a ruled half-sheet of foolscap paper if they cause each successive line to stand for a successive month, beginning from the birth of the child; and if they mark off the measurements by laying, not the 0-inch division of the tape against the edge of the pages, but, say, the 10-inch division—in order to economize space.

The steady and pitiless march of the hidden weaknesses in our constitutions, through illness to death, is painfully revealed by these histories of twins. We are too apt to look upon illness and death as capricious events, and there are some who ascribe them to the direct effect of supernatural interference, whereas the fact of the maladies of two twins being continually alike, shows that illness and death are necessary incidents in a regular sequence of constitutional changes, beginning at birth, upon which external circumstances have, on the whole, very small effect. In cases where the maladies of the twins are continually alike, the clock of life moves regularly on, governed by internal mechanism. When the hand approaches the hour mark, there is a sudden click, followed by a whirling of wheels; at the culminating moment, the stroke falls. Necessitarians may derive new arguments from the life histories of twins.

We will now consider the converse side of our subject. Hitherto we have investigated cases where the similarity at first was close, but afterwards became less: now we will examine those in which there was great dissimilarity at first, and will see how far an identity of nurture in childhood and youth tended to assimilate them. As has been already mentioned, there is a large proportion of cases of sharply contrasted characteristics, both of body and mind, among twins. I have twenty such cases, given with much detail. It is a fact, that extreme dissimilarity, such as existed between Esau and Jacob, is a no less marked peculiarity in twins of the same sex, than extreme similarity. On this curious point, and on much else in the history of twins, I have many remarks to make, but this is not the place to make them.

The evidence given by the twenty cases above mentioned is absolutely accordant, so that the character of the whole may be exactly conveyed by two or three quotations. One parent says: "They have had *exactly the same nurture* from their birth up to the present time; they are both perfectly healthy and strong, yet they are otherwise as dissimilar as two boys could be, physically, mentally, and in their emotional nature." Here is another case: "I can answer most decidedly that the twins have been perfectly dissimilar in character, habits, and likeness from the moment of their birth to the present time, though they were nursed by the same woman, went to school together, and were never separated till the age of fifteen." Here again is one more, in which the father remarks: "They were curiously different in body and mind from their birth." The surviving twin (a senior wrangler of Cambridge) adds: "A fact struck all our school contemporaries, that my brother and I were complementary, so to speak, in point of ability and disposition. He was contemplative, poetical, and literary to a remarkable degree, showing great power in that line. I was practical, mathematical, and linguistic. Between us we should have made a very decent sort of a man." I could quote others just as strong as these, while I have not a single case in which my correspondents speak of originally dissimilar characters having become assimilated through identity of nurture. The impression that all this evidence leaves on the mind is one of some wonder whether nurture can do anything at all beyond giving instruction and professional training. It emphatically corroborates and goes far beyond the conclusions to which we had already been driven by the cases of similarity. In these, the causes of divergence began to act about the period of adult life, when the characters had become somewhat fixed; but here the causes conducive to assimilation began to act from the earliest moment of the existence of the twins, when the disposition was most pliant, and they were continuous until the period of adult life. There is no escape from the conclusion that nature prevails enormously over nurture when the differences of nurture do not exceed what is commonly to be found among persons of the same rank of society and in the same country. My only fear is that my evidence seems to prove too much and may be discredited on that account, as it seems contrary to all experience that nurture should go for little. But experience is often fallacious in ascribing great effects to trifling circumstances. Many a person has amused himself with throwing bits of stick into a tiny brook and watching their progress; how they are arrested, first by one chance obstacle, then by another; and again, how their onward course is facilitated by a combination of circumstances. He might ascribe much importance to each of these events, and think how largely the destiny of the stick has been governed by a series of trifling accidents. Nevertheless all the sticks succeed in passing down the current, and they travel, in the long run, at nearly the same rate. So it is with life in respect to the several accidents which seem to have had a great effect upon our careers. The one element, which varies in different individuals, but is constant in each of them, is the natural tendency; it corresponds to the current in the stream, and invariably asserts itself. More might be added on this matter, and much might be said in qualification of the broad conclusions to which we have arrived, as to the points in which education appears to create the most permanent effect; how far by training the intellect and how far by subjecting the boy to a higher or lower tone of public opinion; but this is foreign to my immediate object. The latter has been to show broadly, and, I trust, convincingly, that statistical estimation of natural gifts by a comparison of successes in life, is not open to the objection stated at the beginning of this memoir. We have only to take reasonable care in selecting our statistics, and then we may safely ignore the many small differences in nurture which are sure to have characterized each individual case.

SIGHT IN SAVAGES

From "Idle Days in Patagonia"

Top

WILLIAM HENRY HUDSON

[William Henry Hudson was born and for many years resided in Patagonia. His "The Naturalist in La Plata" and "Idle Days in Patagonia," both published by J. M. Dent & Co., London, and D. Appleton & Co., New York, are among the most delightful books of natural history ever written.]

A person much given to card-playing once informed me that always after the first few rounds of a game he knew some of the cards in the pack, and could recognize them as they were being dealt out, by means of certain slight shades of difference in the colouring of the backs. He had turned his attention to this business when very young, and as he was close upon fifty when he imparted this interesting piece of information, and had always existed comfortably on his winnings, I saw no reason to disbelieve what he told me. Yet this very man, whose vision was keen enough to detect differences in cards so slight that another could not see them, even when pointed out—this preternaturally sharp-eyed individual was greatly surprised when I explained to him that half a dozen birds of the sparrow kind, that fed in his courtyard, and sang and built their nests in his garden and vineyard and fields, were not one but six distinct species. He had never seen any difference in them: they all had the same customs, the same motions; in size, colour, and shape they were all one; to his hearing they all chirped and twittered alike, and warbled the same song.

And as it was with this man, so, to some extent, it is with all of us. That special thing which interests us, and in which we find our profit or pleasure, we see very distinctly, and our memories are singularly tenacious of its image; while other things, in which we take only a general interest, or which are nothing to us, are not seen so sharply, and soon become blurred in memory; and if there happens to be a pretty close resemblance in several of them, as in the case of my gambling friend's half a dozen sparrows, which, like snowflakes, were "seen rather than distinguished," this indistinctness of their images on the eye and the mind causes them all to appear alike. We have, as it were, two visions—one to which all objects appear vividly and close to us, and are permanently photographed on the mind; the other which sees things at a distance, and with that indistinctness of outline and uniformity of colour which distance gives.

In this place I had proposed to draw on my La Plata notebooks for some amusing illustrations of this fact of our two sights; but it is not necessary to go so far afield for illustrations, or to insist on a thing so familiar. "The shepherd knows his sheep," is a saying just as true of this country—of Scotland, at all events—as of the far East. Detectives, also military men who take an interest in their profession, see faces more sharply than most people, and remember them as distinctly as others remember the faces of a very limited number of individuals—of those they love or fear or constantly associate with. Sailors see atmospheric changes which are not apparent to others; and, in like manner, the physician detects the signs of malady in faces which to the uninstructed vision seem healthy enough. And so on through the whole range of professions and pursuits which men have: each person inhabits a little world of his own, as it were, which to others is only part of the distant general blueness obscuring all things, but in which, to him, every object stands out with wonderful clearness, and plainly tells its story.

All this may sound very trite, very trivial and matter of common knowledge—so common as to be known to every schoolboy and to the boy that goeth not to school; yet it is because this simple familiar fact has been ignored, or has not always been borne in mind by our masters, that they have taught us an error, namely, that savages are our superiors in visual power, and that the difference is so great that ours is a dim decaying sense compared with their brilliant faculty, and that only when we survey the prospect through powerful field-glasses do we rise to their level and see the world as they see it. The truth is that the savage sight is no better than ours, although it might seem natural enough to think the contrary, on account of their simple natural life in the desert, which is always green and restful to the eye, or supposed to be so; and because they have no gas nor even candlelight to irritate the visual nerve, and do themselves no injury by poring over miserable books.

Possibly, then, the beginning of the error was in this preconceived notion, that greenness and the absence of artificial light, with other conditions of a primitive life, kept the sight from deteriorating. The eye's adaptiveness did not get sufficient credit. We know how the muscles may be developed by training, that the blacksmith and prizefighter have mightier arms than others; but it was perhaps assumed that the complex structure and extreme delicacy of the eye would make it less adaptive than other and coarser organs. Whatever the origin of the error may have been, it is certain that it has received the approval of scientists, and that they never open their lips on the subject except to give it fresh confirmation. Their researches have brought to light a great variety of eye-troubles, which, in many cases, are not troublesome at all, until they are discovered, named with a startling name and described in terms very alarming to persons of timid character. Frequently they are not maladies, but inherited defects, like bandy legs, prominent teeth, crushed toes, tender skin and numberless other malformations. That such eye-defects are as common among savages as among ourselves, I do not say, and to this matter I shall return later on; but until the eyes of savages are scientifically examined, it seems a very bold thing to say that defective colour-sense is due to the inimical conditions of our civilization; for we know as little about the colour-sense of savages as we do about the colour-sense of the old Greeks. That the savage sight is vastly more powerful than ours was perhaps not so bold a thing to say, seeing that in this matter our teachers were misled by travellers' tales, and perhaps by other considerations, as, for instance, the absence of artificial aids to sight among the children of nature. The redskin may be very old, but as he sits sunning himself before his wigwam in the early morning he is never observed to trombone his newspaper.

The reader may spare himself the trouble of smiling, for this is not mere supposition; in this case observation came first and reflection afterwards, for I happen to know something of savages from experience, and when they were using their eyes in their way and for their purposes, I used mine for my purpose, which was different. It is true that the redskin will point you out an object in the distance and tell its character, and it will be to your sight only a dark-coloured object, which might be a bush, or stone, or animal of some large kind, or even a house. The secret of the difference is that his eye is trained and accustomed to see certain things, which he looks for and expects to find. Put him where the conditions are new to him and he will be at fault; or even on his native heath, set before him an unfamiliar or unexpected object, and he will show no superiority over his civilized brother. I have witnessed one instance in which not one but five men were all at fault and made a wrong guess; while the one person of our party who guessed correctly, or saw better perhaps, was a child of civilization and a reader of books, and, what is perhaps even more, the descendant of a long line of bookish men. This amazed me at the moment, for until then my childlike faith in the ideas of Humboldt and of the world generally on the subject had never been disturbed. Now I see how this curious thing happened. The object was at such a distance that to all of us alike it presented no definite form, but was merely something dark, standing against a hoary background of tall grass-plumes. Our guides, principally regarding its size, at once guessed it to be an animal which they no doubt expected to find in that place—namely, a wild horse. The other, who did not have that training of the eye and mind for distant objects in the desert which is like an instinct, and, like instinct, is liable to mistakes, and who carefully studied its appearance for himself, pronounced it to be a dark bush. When we got near it turned out to be a clump of tall bulrushes, growing in a place where they had no business to grow, and burnt by drought and frosts to so dark a brown that at a distance they seemed quite black.

In the following case the savage was right. I pointed out an object, dark, far off, so low down as to be just visible above the tall grasses, passing with a falling and rising motion like that of a horseman going at a swinging gallop. "There goes a mounted man," I remarked. "No—a traru," returned my companion, after one swift glance; the traru being a large, black, eagle-like bird of the plains. But the object was not necessarily more distinct to him than to me; he could not see wings and beak at that distance; but the traru was a familiar object, which he was accustomed to see at all distances

—a figure in the landscape which he looked for and expected to find. It was only a dark blot on the horizon; but he knew the animal's habits and appearance, and that when seen far off, in its low down, dilatory rising and falling flight, it simulates the appearance of a horseman in full gallop. To know this and a few other things was his vocation. If one had set him to find a reversed little *s* in the middle of a closely-printed page the tears would have run down his bronzed cheeks, and he would have abandoned the vain quest with aching eyeballs. Yet the proofreader can find the little *s* in a few moments, without straining his sight. But it is infinitely more important to the savage than to us to see things quickly and guess their nature correctly. His daily food, the recovery of his lost animals and his personal safety depend on it; and it is not, therefore, strange that every blot of dark colour, every moving and motionless object on the horizon tells its story better to him than to a stranger; especially when we consider how small a variety of objects he is called on to see and judge of in the level monotonous region he inhabits.

This quick judging of dimly seen distant things, the eye and mind achievement of the mounted barbarian on the unobstructed plains, is not nearly so admirable as that of his fellow-savage in sub-tropical regions overspread with dense vegetation, with animal life in great abundance and variety and where half the attention must be given to species dangerous to man, often very small in size. In some hot humid forest districts, the European who should attempt to hunt or explore with bare feet and legs would be pricked or lacerated at almost every step of his progress, and probably get bitten by a serpent before the day's end. Yet the Indian passes his life there and, naked or half-naked, explores the unknown wilderness of thorns and has only his arrows to provide food for himself and his wife and children. He does not get pierced with thorns and bitten by serpents, because his eye is nicely trained to pick them out in time to save himself. He walks rapidly, but he knows every shade of green, every smooth and crinkled leaf in that dense tangle, full of snares and deceptions, through which he is obliged to walk; and much as leaf resembles leaf, he sets his foot where he can safely set it, or, quickly choosing between two evils, where the prickles and thorns are tenderest, or, for some reason known to him, hurt least. In like manner he distinguishes the coiled-up venomous snake, although it lies so motionless—a habit common to the most deadly kinds—and in its dull imitative colouring is so difficult to be distinguished on the brown earth, and among gray sticks and sere and variegated leaves.

A friend of mine, Fontana of Buenos Ayres, who has a life-long acquaintance with the Argentine Indians, expresses the opinion that at the age of twelve years the savage of the Pampas has completed his education and is thereafter able to take care of himself; but that the savage of the Gran Chaco—the sub-tropical Argentine territory bordering on Paraguay and Bolivia,—if left to shift for himself at that age would speedily perish, since he is then only in the middle of his long, difficult and painful apprenticeship. It was curious and pitiful, he says, to see the little Indian children in the Chaco, when their skins were yet tender, stealing away from their mother and trying to follow the larger ones playing at a distance. At every step they would fall and get pricked with thorns or cut with sharp-edged rushes and tangled in the creepers, and hurt and crying they would struggle on and in this painful manner at last learn where to set their feet.

The snake on the ground, coloured like the ground and shaped like the dead curved sticks or vines seen everywhere on the ground, and motionless like the vine, does not more closely assimilate to its surroundings than birds in trees often do—the birds which the Indian must also see. A stranger in these regions, even the naturalist with a sight quickened by enthusiasm, finds it hard to detect a parrot in a lofty tree, even when he knows that parrots are there; for their greenness in the green foliage and the correlated habit they possess of remaining silent and motionless in the presence of an intruder, make them invisible to him, and he is astonished that the Indian should be able to detect them. The Indian knows how to look for them; it is his trade, which is long to learn; but he is obliged to learn it, for his success in life, and even life itself, depends on it, since in the savage state Nature kills those who fail in her competitive examinations.

The reader has doubtless often seen those little picture-puzzles, variously labelled "Where's the Cat?" or "Mad Bull," or "Burglar," or "Policeman," or "Snake in the Grass," etc., in which the thing named and to be discovered is formed by branches and foliage and by running water and drapery and lights and shadows in the sketch. At first one finds it extremely difficult to detect this picture within a picture; and at last, with the suddenness with which one invariably detects a dull-coloured snake, seen previously but not distinguished—the object sought for appears, and is thereafter so plain to the eye that one cannot look at the sketch, even held at a distance, without seeing the cat or policeman, or whatever it happens to be. And after patiently studying some scores or hundreds of these puzzles one gets to know just how to find the thing concealed, and finds it quickly—almost at a glance at last. Now, the ingenious person that first invented this pretty puzzle probably had no thought of Nature, with her curious imitative and protective resemblances, in his mind; yet he might very well have taken the hint from Nature, for this is what she does. The animal that must be seen to be avoided, and the animal that must be seen to be taken, are there in her picture, sketched in with such cunning art that to the uninstructed eye they form only portions of branch and foliage and shadow and sunlight above, and dull-hued or variegated earth and stones and dead and withering herbage underneath.

It is possible that slight differences may exist in the seeing powers of different nations, due to the effect of physical conditions: thus, the inhabitants of mountainous districts and of dry elevated tablelands may have a better sight than dwellers in low, humid and level regions, although just the reverse may be the case. Among European nations the Germans are generally supposed to have weak eyes, owing, some imagine, to their excessive indulgence in tobacco, while others attribute the supposed decay to the form of type used in their books, which requires closer looking at than ours in reading. That they will deteriorate still further in this direction, and from being a spectacled people become a blind one, to the joy of their enemies, is not likely to happen, and probably the decadence has been a great deal exaggerated. Animals living in darkness become near-sighted, and then nearer-sighted still and so on progressively until the vanishing point is reached. In a community or nation a similar decline might begin from much reading of German books, or perpetual smoking of pipes with big china bowls, or from some other unknown cause; but the decay could not progress far, because there is nothing in man to take the place of sight, as there is in the blind cave rats and fishes and insects. And if we could survey mankind from China to Peru with all the scientific appliances which are brought to bear on the Board-school children in London and on the nation generally, the differences in the powers of vision in the various races, nations and tribes would probably appear very insignificant. The mistake which eye specialists and writers on the eye make is that they think too much about the eye. When they affirm that the conditions of our civilization are highly injurious to the sight, do they mean all the million conditions or sets of conditions embraced by our system, with the infinite variety of occupations and modes of living which men have, from the lighthouse-keeper to the worker underground, whose day is the dim glimmer of a miner's lamp? "An organ exercised beyond its wont will grow and thus meet increase of demand by increase of supply," Herbert Spencer says; but, he adds, there is a limit soon reached, beyond which it is impossible to go. This increase of demand with us is everywhere—now on this organ and now on that, according to our work and way of life, and the eye is in no worse case than the other organs. There are among us many cases of heart complaint; civilization, in such cases, has put too great a strain on that organ, and it has reached the limit beyond which it cannot go. And so with the eye. The total number of the defective among us is no doubt very large, for we know that our system of life retards—it cannot effectually prevent—the healthy action of natural selection. Nature pulls one way and we pull the other, compassionately trying to save the unfit from the consequences of their unfitness. The humane instinct compels us; but the cruel instinct of the savage, who hates the sick and the unfit as the inferior animals do, is less painful to contemplate than that mistaken or perverted compassion which seeks to perpetuate unfitness, and in the interest of suffering individuals inflicts a lasting injury on the race.

Pelleschi, in his admirable book on the Chaco Indians, says that malformations are never seen in these savages, that physically they are all perfect men; and he remarks that in their exceedingly hard struggle for existence in a thorny wilderness, beset with perils, any bodily defect or ailment would be fatal. And as the eye in their life is the most important organ, it must be an eye without flaw. In this circumstance only do savages differ from us—namely, in the absence or rarity of defective eyes among them; and when those who, like Mr. Brudenell Carter, believe in the decadence of the eye in civilized man quote Humboldt's words about the miraculous sight of South American savages, they quote an error. It is not strange that Humboldt should have fallen into it, for, after all, he had only the means which we all possess of finding out things—a limited sight and a fallible mind. Like the savage, he had trained his faculties to observe and infer, and his inferences like those of the savages, were sometimes wrong.

The savage sight is no better than ours for the simple reason that a better is not required. Nature has given to him, as to all her creatures, only what was necessary and nothing for ostentation. Standing on the ground, his horizon is a limited one; and the animals he preys on, if often sharper-eyed and swifter than he, are without intelligence, and thus things are made equal. He can see the rhea as far as the rhea can see him; and if he possessed the eagle's far-seeing faculty it would be of no advantage to him. The high-soaring eagle requires to see very far, but the low-flying owl is near-sighted. And so on through the whole animal world: each kind has sight sufficient to find its food and escape from its enemies, and nothing beyond. Animals that live close to the surface have a very limited sight. Moreover, other faculties may usurp the eye's place, or develop so greatly as to make the eye of only secondary importance as an organ of intelligence. The snake offers a curious case. No other sense seems to have developed in it, yet I take the snake to be one of the nearest-sighted creatures in existence. From long observation of them I am convinced that small snakes of very sluggish habits do not see distinctly farther than from one to three yards. But the snake is the champion faster in the animal world and can afford to lie quiescent until the wind of chance blows something eatable in its way; hence it does not require to see an object distinctly until almost within striking distance. Another remarkable case is that of the armadillo. Of two species I can confidently say that, if they are not blind, they are next door to blindness; yet they are diurnal animals that go abroad in the full glare of noon and wander far in search of food. But their sense of smell is marvellously acute, and, as in the case of the mole, it has made sight superfluous. To come back to man: if, in a state of nature, he is able to guess the character of objects nine times in ten, or nineteen in twenty, seen as far off as he requires to see anything, his intellectual faculties make a better sight unnecessary. If the armadillo's scent had not been so keen and man had not been gifted with nimble brains, the sight in both cases would have been vastly stronger; but the sharpening of its sense of smell has dimmed the armadillo's eyes and made him blinder than a snake; while man (from no fault of his own) is unable to see farther than the wolf and the ostrich and the wild ass.

MECHANISM IN THOUGHT AND MORALS

DR. OLIVER WENDELL HOLMES

[Dr. Holmes was at once a distinguished physician, poet, novelist, and wit. His "Autocrat of the Breakfast Table" is one of the most charming books ever written, his poetry and essays are of even greater popularity. Dr. Holmes's Works are published in fourteen volumes by Houghton, Mifflin & Co., Boston and New York, copyright in various editions. The essay from which extracts follow is in the eighth volume.]

Do we ever think without knowing that we are thinking? The question may be disguised so as to look a little less paradoxical. Are there any mental processes of which we are unconscious at the time, but which we recognize as having taken place by finding certain results in our minds?

That there are such unconscious mental actions is laid down in the strongest terms by Leibnitz, whose doctrine reverses the axiom of Descartes into *I am, therefore I think.* The existence of unconscious thought is maintained by him in terms we might fairly call audacious, and illustrated by some of the most striking facts bearing upon it. The "insensible perceptions," he says, are as important in pneumatology [spiritual philosophy] as corpuscles are in physics.—It does not follow, he says again, that, because we do not perceive thought, it does not exist.—Something goes on in the mind which answers to the circulation of the blood and all the internal movements of the viscera.—In one word, it is a great source of error to believe that there is no perception in the mind but those of which it is conscious.

This is surely a sufficiently explicit and peremptory statement of the doctrine, which, under the names of "latent consciousness," "obscure perceptions," "the hidden soul," "unconscious cerebration," "reflex action of the brain," has been of late years emerging into general recognition in treatises of psychology and physiology.

His allusion to the circulation of the blood and the movements of the viscera, as illustrating his paradox of thinking without knowing it, shows that he saw the whole analogy of the mysterious intellectual movement with that series of reflex actions so fully described half a century later by Hartley, whose observations, obscured by wrong interpretation of the cerebral structure and an insufficient theory of vibrations which he borrowed from Newton, are yet a remarkable anticipation of many of the ideas of modern physiology, for which credit has been given so liberally to Unzer and Prochaska. Unconscious activity is the rule with the actions most important to life. The lout who lies stretched on the tavern bench, with just mental activity enough to keep his pipe from going out, is the unconscious tenant of a laboratory where such combinations are being constantly made as never Wöhler or Berthelot could put together; where such fabrics are woven, such colours dyed, such problems of mechanism solved, such a commerce carried on with the elements and forces of the outer universe, that the industries of all the factories and trading establishments in the world are mere indolence and awkwardness and unproductiveness compared to the miraculous activities of which his lazy bulk is the unheeding centre. All these unconscious or reflex actions take place by a mechanism never more simply stated than in the words of Hartley, as "*vibrations* which ascend up the sensory nerves first, and then are detached down the motory nerves, which communicate with these by some common trunk, plexus, [network] or ganglion [knot]." The doctrine of Leibnitz, that the brain may sometimes act without our taking cognizance of it, as the heart commonly does, as many internal organs always do, seems almost to belong to our time. The readers of Hamilton and Mill, of Abercrombie, Laycock and Maudsley, of Sir John Herschel, of Carpenter, of Lecky, of Dallas, will find many variations on the text of Leibnitz, some new illustrations, a new classification and nomenclature of the facts; but the root of the matter is all to be found in his writings.

I will give some instances of work done in the underground workshop of thought—some of them familiar to the readers of the authors just mentioned. We wish to remember something in the course of conversation. No effort of the will can reach it; but we say, "Wait a minute, and it will come to me," and go on talking. Presently, perhaps some minutes later, the idea we are in search of comes all at once into the mind, delivered like a prepaid bundle, laid at the door of consciousness like a foundling in a basket. How it came there we know not. The mind must have been at work groping and feeling for it in the dark: it cannot have come of itself. Yet, all the while, our consciousness, so far as we are conscious of our consciousness, was busy with other thoughts.

In old persons, there is sometimes a long interval of obscure mental action before the answer to a question is evolved. I remember making an inquiry of an ancient man, whom I met on the road in a waggon with his daughter, about a certain old burial-ground which I was visiting. He seemed to listen attentively; but I got no answer. "Wait half a minute or so," the daughter said, "and he will tell you." And sure enough, after a little time he answered me and to the point. The delay here, probably, corresponded to what machinists call "lost time," or "back lash" in turning an old screw, the thread of which is worn. But, within a fortnight, I examined a young man for his degree in whom I noticed a certain regular interval, and a pretty long one, between every question and its answer. Yet the answer was, in almost every instance, correct, when at last it did come. It was an idiosyncrasy, I found, which his previous instructors had noticed. I do not think the mind knows what it is doing in the interval, in such cases. This latent period, during which the brain is obscurely at work, may, perhaps, belong to mathematicians more than others. Swift said of Sir Isaac Newton that, if one were to ask him a question, "he would revolve it in a circle in his brain, round and round and round" (the narrator here describing a circle on his own fore-head), "before he could produce an answer."

I have often spoken of the same trait in a distinguished friend of my own, remarkable for his mathematical genius, and compared his sometimes long-deferred answer to a question with half a dozen others stratified over it, to the thawing out of the frozen words as told of by Baron Munchausen and Rabelais, and nobody knows how many others before them.

I was told, within a week, of a business man in Boston, who, having an important question under consideration, had given it up for the time as too much for him. But he was conscious of an action going on in his brain which was so unusual and painful as to excite his apprehensions that he was threatened with palsy, or something of that sort. After some hours of this uneasiness, his perplexity was all at once cleared up by the natural solution of his doubt coming to him—worked out, as he believed, in that obscure and troubled interval.

The cases are numerous where questions have been answered, or problems solved, in dreams, or during unconscious sleep. Two of our most distinguished professors in this institution have had such an experience, as they tell me; and one of them has often assured me that he never dreams. Somnambulism and double-consciousness offer another series of illustrations. Many of my audience remember a murder case, where the accused was successfully defended, on the ground of somnambulism, by one of the most brilliant of American lawyers. In the year 1686 a brother of Lord Culpepper was indicted at the Old Bailey for shooting one of the guards and acquitted on the same ground of somnambulism; that is an unconscious and, therefore, irresponsible state of activity.

A more familiar instance of unconscious action is to be found in what we call "absent" persons—those who, while wide awake, act with an apparent purpose, but without really knowing what they are doing; as in La Bruyère's character, who threw his glass of wine into the backgammon board and swallowed the dice.

There are a vast number of movements which we perform with perfect regularity while we are thinking of something quite different—"automatic actions of the secondary kind," as Hartley calls them, and of which he gives various examples. The old woman knits; the young woman stitches, or perhaps plays her piano and yet talks away as if nothing but her tongue were busy. Two lovers stroll along side by side, just born into the rosy morning of their new life, prattling the sweet follies worth all the wisdom that years will ever bring them. How much do they think about that wonderful problem of balanced progression which they solve anew at every step?

We are constantly finding results of unperceived mental processes in our consciousness. Here is a striking instance, which I borrow from a recent number of an English journal. It relates to what is considered the most interesting period of incubation in Sir William Rowan Hamilton's discovery of quaternions. The time was the 15th of October, 1843. On that day, he says in a letter to a friend, he was walking from his observatory to Dublin with Lady Hamilton, when, on reaching Brougham Bridge, he "felt the galvanic circle of thought close; and the sparks that fell from it were the fundamental relations between i, j, k," just as he used them ever afterwards.

Still another instance of the spontaneous evolution of thought we may find in the experience of a great poet. When Goethe shut his eyes and pictured a flower to himself, he says that it developed itself before him in leaves and blossoms. The result of the mental process appeared as pictured thought; but the process itself was automatic and imperceptible.

There are thoughts that never emerge into consciousness, which yet make their influence felt among the perceptible mental currents, just as the unseen planets sway the movements of those which are watched and mapped by the astronomer. Old prejudices that are ashamed to confess themselves nudge our talking thought to utter their magisterial veto. In hours of languor, as Mr. Lecky has remarked in his "History of Rationalism," the beliefs and fancies of obsolete conditions are apt to take advantage of us. We know very little of the contents of our minds until some sudden jar brings them to light, as an earthquake that shakes down a miser's house brings out the old stockings full of gold and all the hoards that have been hidden away in holes and crannies.

We not rarely find our personality doubled in our dreams and do battle with ourselves, unconscious that we are our own antagonists. Dr. Johnson dreamed that he had a contest of wit with an opponent, and got the worst of it: of course he furnished the wit for both. Tartini heard the Devil play a wonderful sonata and set it down on waking. Who was the Devil but Tartini himself? I remember, in my youth, reading verses in a dream, written, as I thought, by a rival fledgling of the Muse. They were so far beyond my powers that I despaired of equalling them; yet I must have made them unconsciously as I read them. Could I only have remembered them waking!

But I must here add another personal experience, of which I will say beforehand—somewhat as honest Isaak Walton said of his pike, "This dish of meat is too good for any but anglers or honest men"—this story is good only for philosophers and very small children. I will merely hint to the former class of thinkers, that its moral bears on two points: first, the value of our self-estimate, sleeping—possibly, also, waking; secondly, the significance of general formulæ when looked at in certain exalted mental conditions.

I once inhaled a pretty full dose of ether, with the determination to put on record, at the earliest moment of regaining consciousness, the thought I should find uppermost in my mind. The mighty music of the triumphal march into nothingness reverberated through my brain, and filled me with a sense of infinite possibilities, which made me an archangel for the moment. The veil of eternity was lifted. The one great truth which underlies all human experience and is the key to all the mysteries that philosophy has sought in vain to solve, flashed upon me in a sudden revelation. Henceforth all was clear: a few words had lifted my intelligence to the level of the knowledge of the cherubim. As my natural condition returned, I remembered my resolution; and, staggering to my desk, I wrote, in ill-shaped, straggling characters, the all embracing truth still glimmering in my consciousness. The words were these (children may smile; the wise will ponder): *"A strong smell of turpentine prevails throughout."*

My digression has served at least to illustrate the radical change which a slight material cause may produce in our thoughts, and the way we think about them. If the state just described were prolonged, it would be called insanity. I have no doubt that there are many ill-organized perhaps over-organized human brains, to which the common air is what the vapour of ether was to mine: it is madness to them to drink in this terrible burning oxygen at every breath; and the atmosphere that enfolds them is like the flaming shirt of Nessus.

The more we examine the mechanism of thought, the more we shall see that the automatic, unconscious action of the mind enters largely into all its processes. Our definite ideas are stepping-stones; how we get from one to the other, we do not know: something carries us; we do not take the step. A creating and informing spirit which is with us, and not of us, is recognized everywhere in real and storied life. It is the Zeus that kindled the rage of Achilles; it is the muse of Homer; it is the Daimon of Socrates; it is the inspiration of the seer; it is the mocking devil that whispers to Margaret as she kneels at the altar; and the hobgoblin that cried, "Sell him, sell him!" in the ear of John Bunyan: it shaped the forms that filled the soul of Michael Angelo when he saw the figure of the great Lawgiver in the yet unhewn marble, and the dome of the world's yet unbuilt basilica against the black horizon; it comes to the least of us, as a voice that will be heard; it tells us what we must believe; it frames our sentences; it lends a sudden gleam of sense or eloquence to the dullest of us all, so that, like Katterfelto with his hair on end, we wonder at ourselves, or rather not at ourselves, but at this divine visitor, who chooses our brain as his dwelling-place, and invests our naked thought with the purple of the kings of speech or song.

After all, the mystery of unconscious mental action is exemplified, as I have said, in every act of mental association. What happens when one idea brings up another? Some internal movement, of which we are wholly unconscious and which we only know by its effect. What is this action, which in Dame Quickly agglutinates contiguous circumstances by their surfaces; in men of wit and fancy, connects remote ideas by partial resemblances; in men of imagination, by the vital identity which underlies phenomenal diversity; in the man of science, groups the objects of thought in sequences of maximum resemblance? Not one of them can answer. There is a Delphi and a Pythoness in every human breast. [At Delphi in ancient Greece was the oracle of Apollo: the Pythoness was his priestess.]

The poet sits down to his desk with an odd conceit in his brain; and presently his eyes fill with tears, his thought slides into the minor key, and his heart is full of sad and plaintive melodies. Or he goes to his work saying "To-night I would have tears," and before he rises from his table he has written a burlesque, such as he might think fit to send to one of the comic papers, if these were not so commonly cemeteries of hilarity interspersed with cenotaphs of wit and humour. These strange hysterics of the intelligence, which make us pass from weeping to laughter, and from laughter back again to weeping, must be familiar to every impressible nature; and all is as automatic, involuntary, as entirely self-evolved by a hidden organic process, as are the changing moods of the laughing and crying woman. The poet always recognizes a dictation from without, and we hardly think it a figure of speech when we talk of his inspiration.

The mental attitude of the poet while writing, if I may venture to define it, is that of the "nun, breathless with adoration." Mental stillness is the first condition of the listening state; and I think my friends the poets will recognize that the sense of effort, which is often felt, accompanies the mental spasm by which the mind is maintained in a state at once passive to the influx from without, and active in seizing only that which will serve its purpose.[3] It is not strange that remembered ideas should often take advantage of the crowd of thoughts and smuggle themselves in as original. Honest thinkers are always stealing unconsciously from each other. Our minds are full of waifs and estrays which we think our own. Innocent plagiarism turns up everywhere. Our best musical critic tells me that a few notes of the air of "Shoo Fly" are borrowed from a movement in one of the magnificent harmonies of Beethoven.

And so the orator—I do not mean the poor slave of a manuscript, who takes his thought chilled and stiffened from its mould, but the impassioned speaker who pours it forth as it flows coruscating from the furnace—the orator only becomes our master at the moment when he himself is surprised, captured, taken possession of, by a sudden rush of fresh inspiration. How well we know the flash of the eye, the thrill of the voice, which are the signature and symbol of nascent thought—thought just emerging into consciousness, in which condition, as is the case with the chemist's elements, it has a combining force at other times wholly unknown!

But we are all more or less improvisators. We all have a double, who is wiser and better than we are, and who puts thoughts into our heads and words into our mouths. Do we not all commune with our own hearts upon our beds? Do we not all divide ourselves and go to buffets on questions of right or wrong, of wisdom or folly? Who or what is it that resolves the stately parliament of the day, with all its forms and conventionalities and pretences, and the great Me presiding, into the committee of the whole, with Conscience in the chair, that holds its solemn session through the watches of the night?

Persons who talk most do not always think most. I question whether persons who think most—that is, have most conscious thought pass through their minds—necessarily do most mental work. The tree that you are sticking in "will be growing when you are sleeping." So with every new idea that is planted in a real thinker's mind: it will be growing when he is least conscious of it. An idea in the brain is not a legend carved on a marble slab: it is an impression made on a living tissue, which is the seat of active nutritive processes. Shall the initials I carved in bark increase from year to year with the tree? and shall not my recorded thought develop into new forms and relations with my growing brain? Mr. Webster told one of our greatest scholars that he had to change the size of his hat every few years. His head grew larger as his intellect expanded. Illustrations of this same fact were shown me many years ago by Mr. Deville, the famous phrenologist, in London. But organic mental changes may take place in shorter spaces of time. A single night of sleep has often brought a sober second-thought, which was a surprise to the hasty conclusion of the day before. Lord Polkommet's description of the way he prepared himself for a judicial decision is in point, except for the alcoholic fertilizer he employed in planting his ideas: "Ye see, I first read a' the pleadings; and then, after letting them wamble in my wame wi' the toddy two or three days, I gie my ain interlocutor."

The problem of memory is closely connected with the question of the mechanical relation between thought and structure. How intimate is the alliance of memory with the material condition of the brain, is shown by the effect of age, of disease, of a blow, of intoxication. I have known an aged person repeat the same question five, six, or seven times during the same brief visit. Everybody knows the archbishop's flavour of apoplexy in the memory as in the other mental powers. I was once asked to see a woman who had just been injured in the street. On coming to herself, "Where am I? What has happened?" she asked. "Knocked down by a horse ma'am; stunned a little: that is all." A pause, "while one with moderate haste might count a hundred," and then again, "Where am I? What has happened?"—"Knocked down by a horse, ma'am; stunned a little: that is all." Another pause, and the same question again; and so on during the whole time I was by her. The same tendency to repeat a question indefinitely has been observed in returning members of those worshipping assemblies whose favourite hymn is "We Won't Go Home Till Morning."

Is memory, then, a material record? Is the brain, like the rocks of the Sinaitic Valley, written all over with inscriptions left by the long caravans of thought, as they have passed year after year through its mysterious recesses?

When we see a distant railway-train sliding by us in the same line, day after day, we infer the existence of a track which guides it. So, when some dear old friend begins that story we remember so well; switching off at the accustomed point of digression; coming to a dead stop at the puzzling question of chronology; off the track on the matter of its being first or second cousin of somebody's aunt; set on it again by the patient, listening wife, who knows it all as she knows her well-worn wedding-ring—how can we doubt that there is a track laid down for the story in some permanent disposition of the thinking-marrow?

I need not say that no microscope can find the tablet inscribed with the names of early loves, the stains left by tears of sorrow or contrition, the rent where the thunderbolt of passion has fallen, or any legible token that such experiences have formed a part of the life of the mortal, the vacant temple of whose thought it is exploring. It is only as an inference, aided by illustration which I will presently offer, that I suggest the possible existence, in the very substance of the brain-tissue, of those inscriptions which Shakespeare must have thought of when he wrote—

> Pluck from the memory a rooted sorrow;
> Raze out the written troubles of the brain.

The objection to the existence of such a material record—that we renew our bodies many scores of times and yet retain our earliest recollections—is entirely met by the fact, that a scar of any kind holds it own nearly through life in spite of all these same changes, as we have not far to look to find instances.

It must be remembered that a billion of the starry brain-cells could be packed in a cubic inch, and that the convolutions contain one hundred and thirty-four cubic inches, according to the estimate already given. My illustration is derived from microscopic photography. I have a glass slide on which there is a minute photographic picture, which is exactly covered when the head of a small pin is laid upon it. In that little speck are clearly to be seen, by a proper magnifying power, the following objects: the Declaration of Independence, with easily recognized facsimile autographs of all the signers; the arms of all the original thirteen States; the Capitol at Washington; and very good portraits of all the Presidents of the United States, from Washington to Mr. James K. Polk. These objects are all distinguishable as a group with a power of fifty diameters: with a power of three hundred any one of them becomes a sizable picture. You may see, if you will, the majesty of Washington on his noble features, or the will of Jackson in those hard lines of the long face crowned with that bristling head of hair in a perpetual state of electrical divergence and centrifugal self-assertion. Remember that each of these faces is the record of a life.

Now recollect that there was an interval between the exposure of the negative in the camera and its development by pouring a wash over it, when all these pictured objects existed potentially, but absolutely invisible and incapable of recognition, in a speck of collodion-film, which a pin's head would cover; and then think what Alexandrian libraries, what Congressional document loads of positively intelligible characters—such as one look of the recording angel would bring out; many of which we can ourselves develop at will, or which come before our eyes unbidden, like "Mene, Mene, Tekel, Upharsin"—might be held in those convolutions of the brain which wrap the talent entrusted to us, too often as the folded napkin of the slothful servant hid the treasure his master had lent him.

Three facts, so familiar that I need only allude to them, show how much more is recorded in the memory than we may ever take cognizance of. The first is the conviction of having been in the same precise circumstances once or many times before. Dr. Wigan says, never but once; but such is not my experience. The second is the panorama of their past lives, said, by people rescued from drowning, to have flashed before them. I had it once myself, accompanied by an ignoble ducking and scrambling self-rescue. The third is the revival of apparently obsolete impressions, of which many strange cases are related in nervous young women and in dying persons, and which the story of the dog Argus in the "Odyssey," and of the parrot so charmingly told by Campbell, would lead us to suppose not of rare occurrence in animals. It is possible, therefore, and I have tried to show that it is not improbable, that memory is a material record; that the brain is scarred and seamed with infinitesimal hieroglyphics, as the features are engraved with the traces of thought and passion. And, if this is so, must not the record, we ask, perish with the organ? Alas! how often do we see it perish *before* the organ!—the mighty satirist tamed into oblivious imbecility; the great scholar wandering without sense of time or place among his alcoves, taking his books one by one from the shelves and fondly patting them; a child once more among his toys, but a child whose to-morrows come hungry, and not full-handed—come as birds of prey in the place of the sweet singers of morning. We must all become as little children if we live long enough; but how blank an existence the wrinkled infant must carry into the kingdom of heaven, if the Power that gave him memory does not repeat the miracle by restoring it!

FOOTNOTES:

[3]Burns tell us how he composed verses for a given tune: "My way is, I consider the poetic sentiment correspondent to my idea of the musical expression; then choose my theme; begin one stanza. When that is composed, which is generally the most difficult part of the business, I walk out, sit down now and then, look out for objects in Nature that are in unison or harmony with the cogitations of my fancy, and workings of my bosom; humming every now and then the air with the verses I have framed. When I feel my Muse beginning to jade I retire to the solitary fireside of my study, and there commit my effusions to paper; swinging at intervals on the hind-legs of my elbow-chair, by way of calling forth my own critical strictures, as my pen goes on."—"Letters to G. Thomson," No. XXXVII.

MEMORY

HENRY MAUDSLEY, M.D.

[Dr. Maudsley, of London, is an eminent physician and psychologist. His works include "Body and Mind," "Body and Will," "Responsibility in Mental Disease," "Pathology of the Mind," all published by D. Appleton & Co., New York. From the work last mentioned the following is part of the chapter on Memory and Imagination.]

No mental development would be possible without memory, for if a man possessed it not he would be obliged to begin his conscious life afresh with each impression made upon him, and would be incapable of any education. We cannot perhaps better define memory than, following Locke, as the power which the mind has "to revive perceptions which it once had with this additional perception annexed to them, that it has had them before;" in other words, as the power or process by which that which has been once known is, when *re*presented to the mind, known as a previous mental experience, that is, is *re*cognized. When people speak of ideas being laid up in the memory, they of course speak metaphorically; there is no such repository in which ideas are stored up, ready to be brought out when required for use; when an idea which we have once had is excited again, there is simply a reproduction of the same nervous current, with the conscious addition that it is a reproduction—it is the same idea *plus* the consciousness that it is the same. The question then suggests itself, What is the physical condition of this consciousness? What is the modification of the anatomical substrata of fibres and cells, or of their physiological activity, which is the occasion of this *plus* element in the reproduced idea? It may be supposed that the first activity did leave behind it, when it subsided, some after-effect, some modification of the nerve element, whereby the nerve circuit was disposed to fall again readily into the same action; such disposition appearing in consciousness as *re*cognition or memory. Memory is, in fact, the conscious phase of this physiological disposition when it becomes active or discharges its functions on the recurrence of the particular mental experience. To assist our conception of what may happen, let us suppose the individual nerve-elements to be endowed with their own consciousness, and let us assume them to be, as I have supposed, modified in a certain way by the first experience; it is hard to conceive that when they fall into the same action on another occasion they should not recognize or remember it; for the second action is a reproduction of the first, with the addition of what it contains from the after-effects of the first. As we have assumed the process to be conscious, this reproduction with its addition would be a memory or remembrance.

Psychology affords us not the least help in this matter, for in describing memory as a faculty of the mind or the conservative faculty it does no more than present us with a name in place of our explanation. But we do get nearer realities when we go down to the organic aptitude which, in consequence of an action, there is to the recurrence of a similar action on another occasion. And physiology presents us with many illustrations of such organized aptitudes. Take, for example, the education of our movements: a designed movement is performed at first slowly and clumsily, and it is only by giving great pains to it and frequently repeating it that we acquire the skill to perform it easily and quickly; the aptitude thereto being at last so completely organized in the proper nervous centres that it may be performed without consciousness on our part, quite automatically. Thus it appears that memory in this case becomes less conscious as it becomes more complete, until, when it has reached its greatest perfection and is performed with the most facility, it is entirely unconscious. After which, if we are psychologists who are content to rest in words and forbear to pursue the facts which they denote, we must cease to speak of it as memory: it has become custom, or habit, or automatism. But if we go beneath words to the property of the motor nerve-centres whereby they react in a definite way to impressions made upon them, organically register their experience, and so acquire by education their special faculties, we perceive that we have not to do in the higher nerve-centres with fundamentally different properties of nerve element, but with different functions which depend upon the same fundamental property. Substitute the highest nerve-centres for the motor nerve-centres, and the complex idea for the complex movement, and what has been said of the latter is strictly true of the former; the idea, like the movement, is accompanied with less consciousness the more completely it is organized, and when it has been completely organized it takes its part automatically in our mental operations, being performed, as a habitual movement is performed, automatically. The physiological condition of memory is, then, the organic process by which nerve-experiences in the different centres are registered; and to recollect is to revive these experiences in the highest centres, the functions of which are attended with consciousness—to stimulate, by external or internal causes, their residua, aptitudes, dispositions, or whatever else we may choose to call them, into functional activity. Stimulated from without, they constitute recognition, that is, cognition with memory of former cognition; stimulated from within, they constitute recollection.

It must be borne in mind, as Dr. Darwin remarked many years ago, that in dealing with memory we have to do not with laws of light, but with laws of life, and that the misleading notion of images or ideas of objects being stored up in the mind has been derived from our experience of the action of light upon the retina. If we would understand the laws of organization in the highest nerve-centres, we shall certainly do well to study organic processes generally; it would be not less absurd to attempt to understand the higher processes without giving attention to the lower, than it would be to attempt to build a house without taking pains to lay its foundations securely. It is a plain matter of observation that other organic elements besides nervous elements perpetuate impressions made upon them, which they may accordingly in a certain sense be said to remember; the virus of smallpox, for example, makes an impression upon all the elements of the body, which they never lose, although it becomes fainter with the lapse of time; in some unknown way it modifies their constitution so that ever afterwards their susceptibilities are changed. The scar which is left after the healing of a wound in a child's finger keeps the same relative proportion to the finger through life, growing as it grows; for the elements of the new tissue not only renew themselves particle by particle, and thus perpetuate it, but they extend it in relation with the growth of the surrounding parts. We need not brave the fire of psychological scorn by calling this retention of impressions *memory*, or care greatly what it is called, so long as due heed is given to the fact; but we may be permitted to perceive in it the same physiological process which, in the cortical [outer] layers of the cerebral [brain's] hemispheres, is the condition of memory, and of habit in thought. Moreover, it may be fairly demanded of the psychologists that they be consistent, and that they no longer use the word memory to denote those mental processes which have been so completely organized that they take place without consciousness; if it be wrong, as they profess, to assume or imply an unconscious memory, it must be still more wrong to assume or imply an unconscious consciousness, as they sometimes do.

In any case, the foregoing considerations cannot fail to show how misleading it is to look upon perceptions as mere pictures of nature, and upon the mind as a vast canvas on which they are cunningly painted; the real process is one of organization, and it is rightly conceivable only by the aid of ideas derived from the observation of organic development—namely, the fundamental ideas of Assimilation of the like and Differentiation of the unlike. Nowhere is it more necessary than in the study of memory to apprehend clearly that what we call mind is the function of a mental organization; for thereby we get rid at once of many empty discussions which have been carried on without definite result; as, for example, whether memory is a knowledge of the past, or a knowledge of the present with a belief of the past, and the like. Moreover, this conception of a mental organization is indispensable to the explanation of the manifold varieties of partial or general loss of memory which are produced by injury, disease and decay of brain; for memory is good or bad according to bodily states, is impaired in various ways by disease, decays with the decay of structure in old age, and is extinguished with the extinction of life in the brain.

From of old two kinds of memory have been distinguished, according as the object remembered occurs to the mind spontaneously, or is voluntarily sought for; the former being known as *memory* proper, the latter as *recollection*. It is certain that we do recognize this difference, which common language attests, between that which is revived without any effort, and that which we endeavour to recover by an effort; and that men differ much, by virtue of natural capacities, both in memory and in power of recollection. No doubt much of the difference in both cases is due to the degree of attention which is given to the subject when it is first presented to the mind, but this will not account satisfactorily for all the difference which is observed; some persons being able to repeat with great ease a row of figures, a number of dates, or several lines of poetry, after reading them over once, while others fail to do so with equal success after reading them over many times. Extraordinary instances have been recorded of this exactness of memory for details reaching back to the earliest periods of life. I have seen an imbecile in the Earlswood Asylum for idiots who can repeat accurately a page or more of any book which he has read years before, even though it was a book which he did not understand in the least; and I once saw an epileptic youth, morally imbecile, who would, shutting his eyes, repeat a leading article in a newspaper word for word, after reading it once. This kind of memory, in which the person seems to read a photographic copy of former impressions with his mind's eye, is not indeed commonly associated with great intellectual power; for what reason I know not, unless it be that the mind to which it belongs is prevented by the very excellence of its power of apprehending and recalling separate facts from rising to that discernment of their higher relations which is involved in reasoning and judgment, and so stays in a function which should be the foundation of its further development; or that, being by some natural defect prevented from rising to the higher sphere of comprehension of relations, it applies all its energies to the apprehension of details. Certainly one runs some risk, by overloading the memory of a child with details, of arresting the development of the mental powers: stereotyping details on the brain, we prevent that further development of it which consists in rising from concrete perception to conception of relations. However, it must be allowed that there have been a few remarkable instances of extraordinary men who have combined a wonderful memory for details with the possession of the highest intellectual powers.

If we now proceed to examine closely the nature of recollection, it will be found that the difference between it and simple memory is not fundamentally so great as appears on the surface. When we voluntarily try hard to remember something which has been forgotten, and succeed in the end, the actual revival is done unconsciously and, as it were, spontaneously;

for it is plain that if we were conscious of what we want we should not need to recollect it, inasmuch as it would already be in possession; and it is furthermore plain that a definite act of volition recalling it must imply a consciousness of it, inasmuch as it is impossible to will what we are not conscious of. Arbitrary recollection by an act of will is therefore nonsense. What we really do when we try to recollect is to apply attention to words or ideas which have, in our past experience, accidental or essential relations to, or associations with, the forgotten word or idea, voluntarily to keep these ideas active by making them consciousness and to trust to their power of awakening into activity that which it is desired to recall; indeed, it is notorious that the best way of succeeding is, having held the related ideas energetically in attention for a time, to allow the thoughts to pass to other things, when the lost idea will, after a longer or shorter time—sometimes indeed after days—recur to the mind. The actual process of reproduction is therefore one of simple or spontaneous memory; we prepare the way for it by stimulating into action the related ideas, but we positively interfere with its success if, by continuing to keep them in attention, we do not permit them to do their work spontaneously; the reason of this being that we thereby hinder the propagation of their activity to other nerve-circuits. We shall understand this the better if we realize that consciousness is the *result* of a certain activity of idea, not driven to it, but drawn by it, and get rid of the metaphysical notion that it is some mysterious power which we direct voluntarily to the idea in order to make it active.

It will not be amiss, before passing from this subject, to take note of and to ponder that certainty which, in trying to recollect something, we have of our possession of what we are thus striving to gain consciously, though we are not conscious what it is. We have the clearest conviction that, although we have forgotten it, we still have it and may recover it. How comes it to pass that we are so sure of the existence of that of which we are not conscious? In the first place, it would appear to supply an argument in support of the theory that something has been left behind in the nerve-circuit ministering to the forgotten idea, in other words, retained by it, which differentiates it from other nerve-circuits, disposes it to a repetition of its former activity, and produces the conviction of a latent possession, even when it is not active, or at any rate not active enough to awaken consciousness. In the second place, it must be remembered that the forgotten idea had associations with other ideas, which are really part of its meaning; it may well be, therefore, that when these are active and occupy the attention, while it remains inactive and below the horizon of consciousness, there is a tendency or sort of effort to reopen the former paths of association, in order to their completeness—to make the circuit, so to speak; and that it is the consciousness of this tendency or effort which gives rise to the certainty which we have of something forgotten. Certain it is, that when a stimulus excites one of two movements which have taken place together or in succession on former occasions, there is a tendency, when the stimulus is powerful or continued, to the reproduction of the associated movement; there is a diffusion of the stimulus along the accustomed path to the associated motor centres, and a union of movements is the result. A piece of poetry which has been thoroughly learnt may be repeated mechanically, as a tune may be whistled, when the proper verbal movements have been once started; indeed, the repetition in such case is most successful when consciousness is not too much occupied with it; for it frequently happens, if we think about the words which we are repeating, we become uncertain and forget, and are obliged, in order to succeed, to begin again and allow the succession of movements to go on automatically. We impede the operation of the spontaneous memory, upon which we really depend, when, by maintaining the activity of a word in consciousness as attention, we hinder the propagation thereof to the associated nerve-circuits.

When a person who is conscious of an idea is striving to revive a related idea which he has forgotten, he presents an example of memory in the making; for he is striving to revive the yet incomplete organic union between them, which was the result of the original apprehension of their relations, and which, when complete, will cause the one idea to recall the other instantly and without the least effort, just as a single sensation of an object at once revives the cluster of sensations which are combined in the perception of it. The process of intellectual development consists in the mental organization of related ideas, as internal representatives of external relations in nature, and in making this organization so complete that a number of associated ideas shall act like a single idea, being combined into a complex product and recalled instantly and without conscious effort, just as a complex movement is. Then the memory is so complete that we must cease to call it memory, because it is unconscious. In fact, spontaneous recollection is at an end when involuntary memory begins, and involuntary memory merges gradually into a reproduction of former mental experiences which is as completely automatic as the habitual movements of our daily life. And well it may be; for the same organic property of nerve element—indeed, I might say, the same fundamental property of organization—is at the bottom of both.

Thus much concerning the nature and function of memory. Upon its basis rests the possibility of mental development, in which there are, as we have already seen, the organic registration of the *simple* ideas of the senses; the assimilation of the like in ideas which takes place in the production or evolution of *general* ideas; the assimilation, of the properties common to two or more general ideas into an *abstract* idea; the special organization or differentiation, or discrimination, of unlike ideas; the organic combination of the ideas derived from the different senses into one *complex* idea, with the further manifold combinations of complex ideas into what Hartley called *duplex* ideas. In fact, no limit is assignable to the complexity of combinations which may go to the formation of a compound idea. Take, for example, the idea of the universe. But how comes it to pass that a new imaginative creation of the mind, to which nothing in nature answers, is effected? By the same process fundamentally as that by which our general and abstract ideas are formed. For when we consider the matter, it appears that there are no actual outside existences answering to our most abstract ideas, which are, therefore, so far new creations of the mind; in their formation there is a blending or coalescence of the like relations in two concrete ideas—the development of a *concept,* there is, as it were, an extraction of the essential out of the particular, a sublimation of the concrete; and, by the creation of a new world in which these essential ideas supersede the concrete ideas, the power of the mind is most largely extended. Now, although there are no concrete objects in nature answering to these abstract ideas, yet these are none the less, when rightly formed, valid and real subjective existences expressing or signifying the essential relations of things, as the flower which crowns development expresses the essential nature of the plant. Thus it is that we rise from the idea of a particular man to the general idea of man, and from that to the abstract idea of virtue as a quality of man; so that for the future we can make use of the abstract idea in all our reasoning, without being compelled to make continual reference to the concrete. Herein, be it remembered again, we have a process corresponding with that which ministers to the production of our motor intuitions; the acquired faculty of certain co-ordinate movements by means of which complicated acts are automatically performed, and we are able to do, almost in the twinkling of an eye, what would cost hours of labour were we compelled on each occasion to go deliberately through the process of special adaptation, is the equivalent, on the motor side, of the general idea by which so much time and labour are saved in reasoning: in both cases there is an internal development in accordance with fundamental laws, and the organized result is, as every new phase of development is, a new creation. Creation is not by fits and starts, but it is continuous in nature.

COMMON SENSE

WILLIAM BOYD CARPENTER, M.D.

[Dr. Carpenter was one of the leading men of science in the generation which has recently passed away. He was a physician and psychologist of mark, and withal a geographer of erudition and extensive travel. His famous work, "Principles of Mental Physiology," is published by D. Appleton & Co., New York. Its eleventh chapter, minus a few paragraphs, is here presented.]

There are two principal forms of common sense which it is desirable clearly to distinguish. The first is what the philosopher means by common sense, when he attributes to it the formation of those original convictions or ultimate beliefs, which cannot be resolved into simpler elements, and which are accepted by every normally constituted human being as direct cognitions of his own mental states. It might, indeed, be maintained that this necessary acceptance of propositions which only need to be intelligibly stated to command unhesitating and universal assent, cannot rightly be termed an act of judgment. But just as sense-perceptions, which are intuitive in the lower animals, have been acquired in man by a process of self-education in the earliest stages, in which acts of judgment are continually called for, so may we regard the autocratic deliverances of the universal common sense of mankind as really having, in the first instance, the characters of true judgments, each expressing the general resultant of uniform experience,—which may be partly of the individual, and partly that of the race embodied in the constitution of each member of it.

The second or popular acceptance of the term common sense, on the other hand, is that of an attribute which judges of things whose self-evidence is not equally apparent to every individual, but presents itself to different individuals in very different degrees, according in part to the original constitution of each, and in part to the range of his experience and degree in which he has profited by it. This is the form of common sense by which we are mainly guided in the ordinary affairs of life: but inasmuch as we no longer find its deliverances in uniform accordance, but encounter continual divergences of judgment as to what things are self-evident,—some being so to A whilst they are not so to B, and others being self-evident to B which are not so to A,—it cannot be trusted as an autocratic or infallible authority. And yet, as Dr. Reid truly says, "disputes very often terminate in an appeal to common sense;" this being especially the case, when to doubt its judgment would be ridiculous.

If the view here taken be correct, these two forms—which may be designated respectively as elementary and as ordinary common sense—have fundamentally the same basis; and we may further connect with them as having a similar genesis, those special forms of common sense, which are the attributes of such as have applied themselves in a scientific spirit to any particular course of inquiry,—things coming to be perfectly self-evident to men of such special culture, which ordinary men, or men whose special culture has lain in a different direction, do not apprehend as such.

The judgment of common sense as to any self-evident truth, may be defined as the immediate or instinctive response that is given (in psychological language) by the automatic action of the mind, or (in physiological language) by the reflex-action of the brain to any question which can be answered by such a direct appeal. The nature and value of that response will depend upon the acquired condition of the mind, or of the brain, at the time it is given; that condition being the general resultant of the whole psychical activity of the individual. The particular form of that activity is determined, as we have seen, in the first place, by his original constitution; secondly, by the influences which have been early brought to bear upon it from without; and thirdly, by his own power of self-direction. And it may be said that while the elementary form of common sense depends mainly upon the first of these factors, its ordinary form chiefly arises out of the first and second, and its special forms almost exclusively out of the third;—the response being given, in each case, by a nervous mechanism, in the organization of which the generalized results of the past experiences of consciousness (whether of the race or of the individual) have become embodied.

The parallel between the cerebral action which furnishes the mechanism of thought now under consideration, and the action of the sensori-motor apparatus which furnishes the mechanism of sense and motion, is extremely close. We have seen that there are certain sense-perceptions, which, although not absolutely intuitive, very early come to possess—in every normally constituted human being—the immediateness and perfection of those corresponding perceptions which are intuitive in the lower animals; and that with these are associated certain respondent motions, which, though acquired by practice in the first instance, ultimately come to be performed as by a second nature. Certain of these motions, such as walking erect, are universally acquired; and thus obviously come to be the expressions of the original endowments of the mechanism, trained by an experience very similar in the uniformity of its character to that which educates the elementary form of common sense. For it must be clear to any one who compares the erect progression of a child who has just learned to walk, with that of a dancing dog or even of a chimpanzee, that while experience makes its acquirement possible in each case, only an organism which is at the same time structurally adapted for erect progression and possessed of a special co-ordinating faculty, can turn such experience to full account. The balancing the body in the erect position at starting, the maintenance of that balance by a new adjustment of the centre of gravity as the base of support is shifted from side to side and from behind forwards, and the alternate lifting and advance of the legs, involve the harmonious co-operation of almost all the muscles in the body. Although this co-operation is brought about in the first instance by the purposive direction of our efforts towards a given end, under the guidance of our visual and muscular sensations, yet when we have once learned to walk erect, we find ourselves able to maintain our balance without any exertion of which we are conscious; all that is necessary for the performance of this movement being that a certain stimulus (volitional, or some other) shall call the mechanism into activity.—But further, we have seen that special powers of sense-perception can be acquired by the habitual direction of the attention to particular classes of objects; and that special movements come to be the secondarily automatic expression of them. How nearly related these are to the preceding, we may assure ourselves by attending to the process by which an adult learns to walk on a narrow base, such as a rope or the edge of a plank. For the co-ordinating action has here to be gone through afresh under altered and more special conditions, so as to give a greater development to the balancing power; yet when this has been fully acquired, it is exerted automatically with such an immediateness and perfection, that a Blondin can cross Niagara on his rope with no more danger of falling into the torrent beneath, than any ordinary man would experience if walking without side-rails along the broad platform of the suspension bridge which spans it. Now since in those cases in which man acquires powers that are original or intuitive in the lower animals, there is the strongest reason for believing that a mechanism forms itself in him which is equivalent to that congenitally possessed by them, we seem fully justified in the belief that in those more special forms of activity which are the result of prolonged training, the sensori-motor apparatus grows to the mode in which it is habitually exercised, so as to become fit for the immediate execution of the mandate it receives: it being often found to act not only without intelligent direction, but without any consciousness of exertion, in immediate response to some particular kind of stimulus,—just as an automaton that executes one motion when a certain spring is touched, will execute a very different one when set going in some other way.

There is strong analogical ground, then, for the belief that the higher part of the nervous mechanism which is concerned in psychical action, will follow the same law; embodying the generalized result of its experiences, so as to become able to evolve, by a direct response, a result of which the attainment originally required the intervention of the conscious mind at several intermediate stages of the process. What there is strong ground for believing in regard to the perceptional consciousness, may fairly be extended to the ideational, which is so intimately connected to it, the unconscious co-ordinating action, which in the former case brings the whole experience to bear upon the question, whilst the decisions of the latter are based upon a limited, and therefore one-sided, view of it,—the defect of judgment being due either to an original want of the co-ordinating power, or to disuse of the exercise of it through the limitation of the attention to special fields of study. It may often be noticed that children display a power of bringing common sense to bear upon the ordinary affairs of life, which seems much beyond that of their elders; and yet a very sensible child will often grow into a much less sensible man. Now the reason of this seems to be, that the child perceives the application of self-evident considerations to the case at issue, without being embarrassed by a number of other considerations (perhaps of a trivial or conventional nature) which distract the attention and unduly influence the judgment of the adult. And the deliverances of a child's common sense thus often resemble those of the old court fools, or jesters, whose function seems to have been to speak out home truths which timid courtiers would not venture to utter. Moreover, as has been well remarked, "it is quite possible for minds of limited power to manage a small range of experience much better than a large, to get confused (as it were) with resources on too great a scale, and therefore to show far more common sense within the comparatively limited field of childish experience, than in the greater world of society or public life. This is probably the explanation of a thing often seen,—how very sagacious people instinctively shrink from a field which their tact tells them is too large for them to manage, and keep to one where they are really supreme."

Now, in so far as our conscious mental activity is under the direction of our will, we can improve this form of common sense, as to both its range and the trustworthiness of its judgments, by appropriate training. Such training, as regards the purely intellectual aspect of common sense, will consist in the determinate culture of the habit of honestly seeking for truth, —dismissing prejudice, setting aside self-interest, searching out all that can be urged on each side of the question at issue, endeavouring to assign to every fact and argument its real value, and then weighing the two aggregates against each other with judicial impartiality. For in proportion to the steadiness with which this course is volitionally pursued, must be its effectiveness in shaping the mechanism whose automatic action constitutes the unconscious thinking, of which the results express themselves in our common-sense judgments.

The ordinary common sense of mankind, disciplined and enlarged by an appropriate culture, becomes one of the most valuable instruments of scientific inquiry; affording in many instances the best and sometimes the only basis for a rational conclusion. A typical case, in which no special knowledge is required, is afforded by the flint implements of the Abbeville and Amiens gravel beds. No logical proof can be adduced that the peculiar shapes of these flints were given to them by human hands; but no unprejudiced person who has examined them now doubts it.

The evidence of design to which, after an examination of one or two such specimens, we should only be justified in attaching a probable value, derives an irresistible cogency from accumulation. On the other hand, the improbability that these flints acquired their peculiar shape by accident, becomes to our minds greater and greater as more and more such specimens are found; until at last this hypothesis, although it cannot be directly disproved, is felt to be almost inconceivable, except by minds previously possessed by the dominant idea of the modern origin of man. And thus what was in the first instance a matter of discussion, has now become one of those self-evident propositions, which claim the unhesitating assent of all whose opinion on the subject is entitled to the least weight.

We proceed upwards, however, from such questions as the common sense of mankind generally is competent to decide, to those in which special knowledge is required to give value to the judgment; and here we must distinguish between those departments of inquiry in which scientific conclusions are arrived at by a process of strict reasoning, and those in which they partake of the nature of common sense judgments.

Of the former class we have a typical example in mathematics, and in those exact sciences which make use of mathematics as their instrument of proof; but even in these, it is common sense which affords not only the basis, but the materials of the fabric. For while the axioms of geometry are self-evident truths which not only do not require proof, but are not capable of being proved in all their universality, every step of a demonstration is an assertion of which our acceptance depends on our incapability of conceiving either the contrary or anything else than the thing asserted. And thus the certain assurance of the proof felt by every person capable of understanding a mathematical demonstration, depends upon the conclusive self-evidence of each step of it. But we not unfrequently meet with individuals, not deficient in ordinary common sense, who cannot be brought to see this self-evidence; whilst, on the other hand, the advanced mathematician, when adventuring into new paths of inquiry, is able to take a great deal for granted as self-evident, which at an earlier stage of his researches would not have so presented itself to his mind. The deliverances of this acquired intuition can in most cases be readily justified by the reasoning process which they have anticipated. But the genius of a mathematician—that is, his special aptitude developed by special culture—will occasionally enable him to divine a truth, of which, though he may be able to prove it experientially, neither he nor any other can at the time furnish a logical demonstration. In this divining power we have clear evidence of the existence of a capacity which cannot be accounted for by the mere co-ordination of antecedent experiences, whether of the individual or of the race; and yet, as already shown, such co-ordination has furnished the stimulus to its development.

Of those departments of science, on the other hand, in which our conclusions rest (like those of ordinary common sense) not on any one set of experiences, but upon our unconscious co-ordination of the whole aggregate of our experiences,—not on the conclusiveness of any one train of reasoning, but on the convergence of all our lines of thought towards one centre,—geology may be taken as a typical example. For this inquiry brings (as it were) into one focus, the light afforded by a great variety of studies,—physical and chemical, geographical and biological; and throws it on the pages of that great stone book in which the past history of our globe is recorded. And its real progress dates from the time when that common sense method of interpretation came to be generally adopted, which consists in seeking the explanation of past changes in the forces at present in operation, instead of invoking (as the older geologists were wont to do) the aid of extraordinary and mysterious agencies.

Of the adequacy of common sense to arrive at a decisive judgment under the guidance of the convergence just indicated, we have a good example in the following occurrence:—A man having had his pocket picked of a purse, and the suspected thief having been taken with a purse upon him, the loser was asked if he could swear to it as his property. This he could not do; but as he was able to name not only the precise sum which the purse contained, but also the pieces of money of which that sum consisted, the jury unhesitatingly assigned to him the ownership of the purse and its contents. A mathematician could have calculated, from the number of coins, what were the chances against the correctness of a mere guess; but no such calculation could have added to the assurance afforded by common sense, that the man who could tell not only the number of coins in the purse, but the value of each one of them, must have been its possessor.

Familiar instances of the like formation of a basis of judgment by the unconscious co-ordination of experiences, will be found in many occurrences of daily life; in which the effect of special training manifests itself in the formation of decisions, that are not the less to be trusted because they do not rest on assignable reasons:—Thus, a literary man, who has acquired by culture the art of writing correctly and forcibly, without having ever formally studied either grammar, the logical analysis of sentences, or the artifices of rhetoric, will continually feel in criticizing his own writings or those of others, that there is something faulty in style or construction, and may be able to furnish the required correction, whilst altogether unable to say in what the passage is wrong, or why his amendment sets it right. Or, to pass into an entirely different sphere, a practised detective will often arrive, by a sort of divination, at a conviction of the guilt or innocence of a suspected person, which ultimately turns out to be correct; and yet he could not convey to another any adequate reasons for his assurance, which depends upon the impression made upon his mind by minute details of look, tone, gesture, or manner, which have little or no significance to ordinary observers, but which his specially cultured common sense instinctively apprehends.

But in the ordinary affairs of life, our common sense judgments are so largely influenced by the emotional part of our nature—our individual likes and dislikes, the predominance of our selfish or of our benevolent affections, and so on,—that their value will still more essentially depend upon the earnestness and persistency of our self-direction towards the right. [4] The more faithfully, strictly, and perseveringly we try to disentangle ourselves from all selfish aims, all conscious prejudices, the more shall we find ourselves progressively emancipated from those unconscious prejudices, which cling around us as results of early misdirection and habits of thought and which (having become embodied in our organization) are more dangerous than those against which we knowingly put ourselves on guard. And so, in proportion to the degree in which we habituate ourselves to try every question by first principles, rather than by the supposed dictates of a temporary expediency, will the mechanism of our unconscious thinking form itself in accordance with those principles, so often as to evolve results which satisfy both ourselves and others with their self-evident truthfulness and rectitude. It has been well remarked by a man of large experience of human nature and action, that the habitual determination to do the right thing, marvellously clears the judgment as to matters purely intellectual or prudential, having in themselves no moral bearing.

Of this we have a good illustration in the advice which an eminent and experienced judge (the story is told of Lord Mansfield) is said to have given to a younger friend, newly appointed to a colonial judgeship:—"Never give reasons for your decisions; your judgments will very probably be right, but your reasons will almost certainly be wrong." The meaning of this may be taken to be:—"Your legal instinct, or specially trained common sense, based on your general knowledge of law, guided by your honesty of intention, will very probably lead you to correct conclusions; but your knowledge of the technicalities of law is not sufficient to enable you to give reasons for these conclusions, which shall bear the test of hostile scrutiny."

But further, in any of those complicated questions that are pretty sure to come before us all at some time or other in our lives,—as to which there is a great deal to be said on both sides; in which it is difficult to say what is prudent and even what is right; in which it is not duty and inclination that are at issue, but one set of duties and inclinations at issue with another,—experience justifies the conclusion to which science seems to point, that the habitually well-regulated mind forms its surest judgment by trusting to the automatic guidance of its common sense; just as a rider who has lost his road is more likely to find his way home by dropping the reins on his horse's neck, than by continuing to jerk them to this side or that in the vain search for it. For continued argument and discussion, in which the feelings are excited on one side, provoke antagonistic feelings on the other; and no true balance can be struck until all these adventitious influences have ceased to operate. When all the considerations which ought to be taken into the account have been once brought fully before the mind, it is far better to leave them to arrange themselves, by turning the conscious activity of the mind into some other direction, or by giving it a complete repose. If adequate time be given for this unconscious co-ordination, which is especially necessary when the feelings have been strongly and deeply moved, we find, when we bring the question again under consideration, that the direction in which the mind gravitates is a safer guide than any judgment formed when we are fresh from its discussion.

Not only may the range and value of such common sense judgments be increased by appropriate culture in the individual, for, of all parts of our higher nature, the aptitude for forming them is probably that which is most capable of being transmitted hereditarily; so that the descendant of a well-educated ancestry constitutionally possesses in it much higher measure than the progeny of any savage race. And it seems to be in virtue of this automatic co-ordination of the elements of judgment, rather than of any process of conscious ratiocination, that the race, like the individual, emancipates itself from early prejudices, gets rid of worn-out beliefs, and learns to look at things as they are, rather than as they have been traditionally represented. This is what is really expressed by the progress of rationalism. For although that progress undoubtedly depends in great part upon the more general diffusion of knowledge and the higher culture of those intellectual powers which are exercised in the acquirement of it, yet this alone would be of little avail, if the self-discipline thus exerted did not act downwards in improving the mechanism that evolves the self-evident material of our reasoning processes, as well as upwards in more highly elaborating their product. If we examine, for instance, the history of the decline of the belief in witchcraft, we find that it was not killed by discussion, but perished of neglect. The common sense of the best part of mankind has come to be ashamed of ever having put any faith in things whose absurdity now appears self-evident; no discussion of evidence once regarded as convincing is any longer needed; and it is only among those of our hereditarily uneducated population, whose general intelligence is about on a par with that of a Hottentot or an Esquimaux, that we any longer find such faith entertained.

There is, in fact, a sort of under-current, not of actually formed opinion, but of tendency to the formation of opinions, in certain directions, which bursts every now and then to the surface; exhibiting a latent preparedness in the public mind to look at great questions in a new point of view, which leads to most striking results when adequately guided. That "the hour is come—and the man" is what history continually reproduces; neither can do anything effectively without the other. But a great idea thrown out by a mind in advance of its age, takes root and germinates in secret, shapes the unconscious thought of a few individuals of the next generation, is by them diffused still more widely, and thus silently matures itself in the womb of time, until it comes forth, like Minerva, in full panoply of power.

Those who are able to look back with intelligent retrospect over the political history of the last half-century and who witness the now general pervasion of the public mind by truths which it accepts as self-evident, and by moral principles which it regards as beyond dispute, can scarcely realize to themselves the fact that within their own recollection the fearless assertors of those truths and principles were scoffed at as visionaries or reviled as destructives. And those whose experience is limited to a more recent period, must see, in the rapid development of public opinion on subjects of the highest importance, the evidence of a previous unconscious preparedness, which may be believed to consist mainly in the higher development and more general diffusion of that automatic co-ordinating power, which constitutes the essence of reason as distinct from reasoning.

Thus, then, every course of intellectual and moral self-discipline, steadily and honestly pursued, tends not merely to clear the mental vision of the individual, but to ennoble the race; by helping to develop that intuitive power, which arises in the first instance from the embodiment in the human constitution of the general resultants of antecedent experience, but which, in its highest form, far transcends the experience that has furnished the materials for its evolution,—just as the creative power of imagination shapes out conceptions which no merely constructive skill could devise.

FOOTNOTES:

[4] Note by Editor. Sir Henry Taylor in "The Statesman" says:—

"If there be in the character not only sense and soundness, but virtue of a high order, then, however little appearance there may be of talent, a certain portion of wisdom may be relied upon almost implicitly. For the correspondencies of wisdom and goodness are manifold; and that they will accompany each other is to be inferred, not only because men's wisdom makes them good, but also because their goodness makes them wise. Questions of right and wrong are a perpetual exercise of the faculties of those who are solicitous as to the right and wrong of what they do and see; and a deep interest of the heart in these questions carries with it a deeper cultivation of the understanding than can be easily effected by any other excitement to intellectual activity."

A LIBERAL EDUCATION

Top

PROFESSOR T. H. HUXLEY

[In 1868 Professor Huxley delivered an address to the South London Workingmen's College, part of which follows. The address appears in full in the third volume of the author's essays, published by D. Appleton & Co., New York.]

What is education? Above all things, what is our ideal of a thoroughly liberal education?—of that education which, if we could begin life again, we would give ourselves—of that education which, if we could mould the fates to our own will, we would give our children? Well, I know not what may be your conceptions upon this matter, but I will tell you mine, and I hope I shall find that our views are not very discrepant.

Suppose it were perfectly certain that the life and fortune of every one of us would, one day or other, depend upon his losing or winning a game of chess. Don't you think that we should all consider it to be a primary duty to learn at least the names and moves of the pieces; to have a notion of a gambit, and a keen eye for all the means of giving and getting out of check? Do you not think that we should look with a disapprobation amounting to scorn, upon the father who allowed his son, or the State which allowed its members, to grow up without knowing a pawn from a knight?

Yet it is a very plain and elementary truth, that the life, the fortune, and the happiness of every one of us, and, more or less, of those who are connected with us, do depend upon our knowing something of the rules of a game infinitely more difficult and complicated than chess? It is a game which has been played for untold ages, every man and woman of us being one of the two players in a game of his or her own. The chess-board is the world, the pieces are the phenomena of the universe, the rules of the game are what we call the laws of Nature. The player on the other side is hidden from us. We know that his play is always fair, just and patient. But also we know, to our cost, that he never overlooks a mistake, or makes the smallest allowance for ignorance. To the man who plays well, the highest stakes are paid, with that sort of overflowing generosity with which the strong shows delight in strength. And one who plays ill is checkmated—without haste, but without remorse.

My metaphor will remind some of you of the famous picture in which Retzsch has depicted Satan playing at chess with man for his soul. Substitute for the mocking fiend in that picture a calm, strong angel who is playing for love, as we say, and would rather lose than win—and I should accept it as an image of human life.

Well, what I mean by Education is learning the rules of this mighty game. In other words, education is the instruction of the intellect in the laws of Nature, under which name I include not merely things and their forces, but men and their ways; and the fashioning of the affections and of the will into an earnest and loving desire to move in harmony with those laws. For me, education means neither more nor less than this. Anything which professes to call itself education must be tried by this standard, and if it fails to stand the test, I will not call it education, whatever may be the force of authority, or of numbers, upon the other side.

It is important to remember that, in strictness, there is no such thing as an uneducated man. Take an extreme case. Suppose that an adult man, in the full vigour of his faculties, could be suddenly placed in the world, as Adam is said to have been, and then left to do as he best might. How long would he be left uneducated? Not five minutes. Nature would begin to teach him, through the eye, the ear, the touch, the properties of objects. Pain and pleasure would be at his elbow telling him to do this and avoid that; and by slow degrees the man would receive an education which, if narrow, would be thorough, real, and adequate to his circumstances, though there would be no extras and very few accomplishments.

And if to this solitary man entered a second Adam, or, better still, an Eve, a new and greater world, that of social and moral phenomena, would be revealed. Joys and woes, compared with which all others would seem but faint shadows, would spring from the new relations. Happiness and sorrow would take the place of the coarser monitors, pleasure and pain; but conduct would still be shaped by the observation of the natural consequences of actions; or, in other words, by the laws of the nature of man.

To every one of us the world was once as fresh and new as to Adam. And then, long before we were susceptible of any other modes of instruction, Nature took us in hand, and every minute of waking life brought its educational influence, shaping our actions into rough accordance with Nature's laws, so that we might not be ended untimely by too gross disobedience. Nor should I speak of this process of education as past for any one, be he as old as he may. For every man the world is as fresh as it was at the first day, and as full of untold novelties for him who has the eyes to see them. And Nature is still continuing her patient education of us in that great university, the universe, of which we are all members.

Those who take honours in Nature's university, who learn the laws which govern men and things and obey them, are the really great and successful men in this world. The great mass of mankind are the "Poll," who pick up just enough to get through without much discredit. Those who won't learn at all are plucked; and then you can't come up again. Nature's pluck means extermination.

Thus the question of compulsory education is settled so far as Nature is concerned. Her bill on that question was framed and passed long ago. But, like all compulsory legislation, that of Nature is harsh and wasteful in its operation. Ignorance is visited as sharply as wilful disobedience—incapacity meets with the same punishment as crime. Nature's discipline is not even a word and a blow, and the blow first; but the blow without the word. It is left to you to find out why your ears are boxed.

The object of what we commonly call education—that education in which man intervenes and which I shall distinguish as artificial education—is to make good these defects in Nature's methods; to prepare the child to receive Nature's education, neither incapably nor ignorantly, nor with wilful disobedience; and to understand the preliminary symptoms of her pleasure, without waiting for the box on the ear. In short, all artificial education ought to be an anticipation of natural education. And a liberal education is an artificial education which has not only prepared a man to escape the great evils of disobedience to natural laws, but has trained him to appreciate and to seize upon the rewards, which Nature scatters with as free a hand as her penalties.

That man, I think, has had a liberal education who has been so trained in youth that his body is the ready servant of his will, and does with ease and pleasure all the work that, as a mechanism, it is capable of; whose intellect is a clear, cold, logic engine, with all its parts of equal strength, and in smooth working order; ready, like a steam engine, to be turned to any kind of work and spin the gossamers as well as forge the anchors of the mind; whose mind is stored with a knowledge of the great and fundamental truths of Nature and of the laws of her operations; one who, no stunted ascetic, is full of life and fire, but whose passions are trained to come to heel by a vigorous will, the servant of a tender conscience; who has learned to love all beauty, whether of Nature or of art, to hate all vileness, and to respect others as himself.

Such an one and no other, I conceive, has had a liberal education; for he is, as completely as a man can be, in harmony with Nature. He will make the best of her, and she of him. They will get on together rarely; she as his ever beneficent mother; he as her mouthpiece, her conscious self, her minister and interpreter.

[Then follows an account of English primary schools in 1868, setting forth defects many of which have since been removed.]

Least of all, does the child gather from this primary "education" of ours a conception of the laws of the physical world, or of the relations of cause and effect therein. And this is the more to be lamented, as the poor are especially exposed to physical evils, and are more interested in removing them than any other class of the community. If any one is concerned in knowing the ordinary laws of mechanics one would think it is the hand-labourer, whose daily toil lies among levers and pulleys; or among the other implements of artisan work. And if any one is interested in the laws of health, it is the poor workman, whose strength is wasted by ill-prepared food, whose strength is sapped by bad ventilation and bad drainage, and half whose children are massacred by disorders which might be prevented. Not only does our present primary education carefully abstain from hinting to the workman that some of his greatest evils are traceable to mere physical agencies, which could be removed by energy, patience, and frugality; but it does worse—it renders him, so far as it can, deaf to those who could help him, and tries to substitute an Oriental submission to what is falsely declared to be the will of God, for his natural tendency to strive after a better condition.

What wonder, then, if very recently an appeal has been made to statistics for the profoundly foolish purpose of showing that education is of no good—that it diminishes neither misery nor crime among the masses of mankind? I reply, why should the thing which is called education do either the one or the other? If I am a knave or a fool, teaching me to read or write won't make me less of either one or the other—unless somebody shows me how to put my reading and writing to wise and good purposes.

Suppose any one were to argue that medicine is of no use, because it could be proven statistically, that the percentage of deaths was just the same among people who had been taught how to open a medicine chest, and among those who did not so much as know the key by sight. The argument is absurd; but it is not more preposterous than that against which I am contending. The only medicine for suffering, crime, and all the other woes of mankind, is wisdom. Teach a man to read and write, and you have put into his hands the great keys of the wisdom box. But it is quite another matter whether he ever opens the box or not. And he is as likely to poison as to cure himself, if, without guidance, he swallows the first drug that comes to hand. In these times a man may as well be purblind, as unable to read— lame, as unable to write. But I protest that, if I thought the alternative were a necessary one, I would rather that the children of the poor should grow up ignorant of both these mighty arts than that they should remain ignorant of that knowledge to which these arts are means.

It may be said that all these animadversions may apply to primary schools, but that the higher schools, at any rate, must be allowed to give a liberal education. In fact they professedly sacrifice everything else to this object.

Let us inquire into this matter. What do the higher schools, those to which the great middle-class of the country sends its children, teach, over and above the instruction given in the primary schools? There is a little more reading and writing of English. But, for all that, every one knows that it is a rare thing to find a boy of the middle or upper classes who can read aloud decently, or who can put his thoughts on paper in clear and grammatical (to say nothing of good or elegant) language. The "ciphering" of the lower schools expands into elementary mathematics in the higher; into arithmetic, with a little algebra, a little Euclid. But I doubt if one boy in five hundred has ever heard the explanation of a rule of arithmetic, or knows his Euclid otherwise than by rote.

Of theology, the middle-class schoolboy gets rather less than poorer children, less absolutely and less relatively, because there are so many other claims upon his attention. I venture to say that, in the great majority of cases, his ideas on this subject when he leaves school are of the most shadowy and vague description, and associated with painful impressions of the weary hours spent in learning collects and catechism by heart.

Modern geography, modern history, modern literature; the English language as a language; the whole circle of the sciences, physical, moral, and social, are even more completely ignored in the higher than in the lower schools. Up till within a few years back a boy might have passed through any one of the great public schools with the greatest distinction and credit, and might never so much as have heard of the subjects I have just mentioned. He might never have heard that the earth goes round the sun; that England underwent a great revolution in 1688, and France another in 1789; that there once lived certain notable men called Chaucer, Shakespeare, Milton, Voltaire, Goethe, Schiller. The first might be a German and the last an Englishman for anything he could tell you to the contrary. And as for science, the only idea the word would suggest to his mind would be dexterity in boxing.

I have said that this was the state of things a few years back, for the sake of the few righteous who are to be found among the educational cities of the plain. But I would not have you too sanguine about the result, if you sound the minds of the existing generation of public schoolboys, on such topics as those I have mentioned.

Now let us pause to consider this wonderful state of affairs; for the time will come when Englishmen will quote it as the stock example of the stolid stupidity of their ancestors in the nineteenth century. The most thoroughly commercial people, the greatest voluntary wanderers and colonists the world has ever seen, are precisely the middle class of this country. If there be a people which has been busy making history on the great scale for the last three hundred years—and the most profoundly interesting history—history which, if it happened to be that of Greece or Rome, we should study with avidity—it is the English. If there be a people which, during the same period, has developed a remarkable literature, it is our own. If there be a nation whose prosperity depends absolutely and wholly upon their mastery over the forces of Nature, upon their intelligent apprehension of and obedience to the laws of the creation and distribution of wealth, and of the stable equilibrium of the forces of society, it is precisely this nation. And yet this is what these wonderful people tell their sons:—"At the cost of from one to two thousand pounds of our hard-earned money, we devote twelve of the most precious years of your lives to school. There you shall toil, or be supposed to toil; but there you shall not learn one single thing of all those you will most want to know directly you leave school and enter upon the practical business of life. You will in all probability go into business, but you shall not know where, or how, any article of commerce is produced, or the difference between an export or an import, or the meaning of the word 'capital.' You will very likely settle in a colony, but you shall not know whether Tasmania is part of New South Wales or *vice versa*.

"Very probably you may become a manufacturer, but you shall not be provided with the means of understanding the working of one of your own steam engines, or of the nature of the raw products you employ; and, when you are asked to buy a patent, you shall not have the slightest means of judging whether the inventor is an impostor who is contravening the elementary principles of science, or a man who will make you as rich as Crœsus.

"You will very likely get into the House of Commons. You will have to take your share in making laws which may prove a blessing or a curse to millions of men. But you shall not hear one word respecting the political organization of your country; the meaning of the controversy between free-traders and protectionists shall never have been mentioned to you; you shall not so much as know that there are any such things as economical laws.

"The mental power which will be of most importance in your daily life will be the power of seeing things as they are without regard to authority; and of drawing accurate general conclusions from particular facts. But at school and at college you shall know of no source of truth but authority; nor exercise your reasoning faculty upon anything but deduction from what is laid down by authority.

"You will have to weary your soul with work, and many a time eat your bread in sorrow and in bitterness, and you shall not have learned to take refuge in the great source of pleasure without alloy, the serene resting-place for worn human nature,—the world of art."

Said I not rightly that we are a wonderful people? I am quite prepared to allow that education entirely devoted to these omitted subjects might not be a completely liberal education. But is an education which ignores them all a liberal education? Nay, is it too much to say that the education which should embrace these subjects and no others would be a real education, though an incomplete one; while an education which omits them is really not an education at all, but a more or less useful course of intellectual gymnastics?

For what does the middle-class school put in the place of all these things which are left out? It substitutes what is usually comprised under the compendious title of the "classics"—that is to say, the languages, the literature and the history of the ancient Greeks and Romans, and the geography of so much of the world as was known to these two great nations of antiquity. Now, do not expect me to depreciate the earnest and enlightened pursuit of classical learning. I have not the least desire to speak ill of such occupations, nor any sympathy with them who run them down. On the contrary, if my opportunities had lain in that direction, there is no investigation into which I could have thrown myself with greater delight than that of antiquity.

What science can present greater attractions than philology? How can a lover of literary excellence fail to rejoice in the ancient masterpieces? And with what consistency could I, whose business lies so much in the attempt to decipher the past and to build up intelligible forms out of the scattered fragments of long-extinct beings, fail to take a sympathetic, though an unlearned, interest in the labours of a Niebuhr, a Gibbon, or a Grote? Classical history is a great section of the palæontology of man; and I have the same double respect for it as for other kinds of palæontology—that is to say, a respect for the facts which it establishes as for all facts, and a still greater respect for it as a preparation for the discovery of a law of progress.

But if the classics were taught as they might be taught—if boys and girls were instructed in Greek and Latin, not merely as languages, but as illustrations of philological science; if a vivid picture of life on the shores of the Mediterranean two thousand years ago were imprinted on the minds of scholars; if ancient history were taught, not as a weary series of feuds and fights, but traced to its causes in such men placed under such conditions; if, lastly, the study of classical books were followed in such a manner as to impress boys with their beauties and with the grand simplicity of their statement of the everlasting problems of human life, instead of with their verbal and grammatical peculiarities; I still think it as little proper that they should form the basis of a liberal education for our contemporaries, as I should think it fitting to make that sort of palæontology with which I am familiar the back-bone of modern education.

It is wonderful how close a parallel to classical training could be made out of that palæontology to which I refer. In the first place I could get up an osteological primer so arid, so pedantic in its terminology, so altogether distasteful to the youthful mind, as to beat the recent famous production of the head-masters out of the field in all these excellences. Next, I could exercise my boys upon easy fossils and bring out all their powers of memory and all their ingenuity in the application of my osteo-grammatical rules to the interpretation, or construing, of those fragments. To those who had reached the higher classes, I might supply odd bones to be built up into animals, giving great honour and reward to him who succeeded in fabricating monsters most entirely in accordance with the rules. That would answer to verse-making and essay-writing in the dead languages.

To be sure, if a great comparative anatomist were to look at these fabrications he might shake his head or laugh. But what then? Would such a catastrophe destroy the parallel? What, think you, would Cicero or Horace say to the production of the best sixth form going? And would not Terence stop his ears and run out if he could be present at an English performance of his own plays? Would Hamlet, in the mouths of a set of French actors, who should insist on pronouncing English after the fashion of their own tongue, be more hideously ridiculous?

But it will be said that I am forgetting the beauty and the human interest which appertain to classical studies. To this I reply that it is only a very strong man who can appreciate the charms of a landscape as he is toiling up a steep hill, along a bad road. What with short-windedness, stones, ruts and a pervading sense of the wisdom of rest and be thankful, most of us have little enough sense of the beautiful under these circumstances. The ordinary schoolboy is precisely in this case. He finds Parnassus uncommonly steep, and there is no chance of his having much time or inclination to look about him till he gets to the top. And nine times out of ten he does not get to the top.

But if this be a fair picture of the results of classical teaching at its best —and I gather from those who have authority to speak on such matters that it is so—what is to be said of classical teaching at its worst, or in other words, of the classics of our ordinary middle-class schools? I will tell you. It means getting up endless forms and rules by heart. It means turning Latin and Greek into English, for the mere sake of being able to do it, and without the smallest regard to the worth, or worthlessness of the author read. It means the learning of innumerable, not always decent, fables in such a shape that the meaning they once had is dried up into utter trash; and the only impression left upon a boy's mind is, that the people who believed such things must have been the greatest idiots the world ever saw. And it means, finally, that after a dozen years spent at this kind of work, the sufferer shall be incompetent to interpret a passage in an author he has not already got up; that he shall loathe the sight of a Greek or Latin book; and that he shall never open, or think of, a classical writer again, until, wonderful to relate, he insists upon submitting his sons to the same process.

Ask the man who is investigating any question profoundly and thoroughly—be it historical, philosophical, philological, physical, literary, or theological; who is trying to make himself master of any abstract subject (except, perhaps, political economy and geology, both of which are intensely Anglican sciences), whether he is not compelled to read half a dozen times as many German as English books? And whether, of these English books, more than one in ten is the work of a fellow of a college, or a professor of an English university?

Is this from any lack of power in the English as compared with the German mind? The countrymen of Grote and of Mill, of Faraday, of Robert Brown, of Lyell and of Darwin, to go no further back than the contemporaries of men of middle age, can afford to smile at such a suggestion. England can show now, as she has been able to show in every generation since civilization spread over the West, individual men who hold their own against the world, and keep alive the old tradition of her intellectual eminence.

But, in the majority of cases, these men are what they are in virtue of their native intellectual force and of a strength of character which will not recognize impediments. They are not trained in the courts of the Temple of Science, but storm the walls of that edifice in all sorts of irregular ways, and with much loss of time and power, in order to obtain their legitimate positions.

Our universities not only do not encourage such men; do not offer them positions in which it should be their highest duty to do, thoroughly, that which they are most capable of doing; but, as far as possible, university training shuts out of the minds of those among them, who are subjected to it, the prospect that there is anything in the world for which they are specially fitted. Imagine the success of the attempt to still the intellectual hunger of any of the men I have mentioned, by putting before him, as the object of existence, the successful mimicry of the measure of a Greek song, or the roll of Ciceronian prose! Imagine how much success would be likely to attend the attempt to persuade such men that the education which leads to perfection in such elegances is alone to be called culture; while the facts of history, the process of thought, the conditions of moral and social existence and the laws of physical nature are left to be dealt with as they may by outside barbarians!

It is not thus that the German universities, from being beneath notice a century ago, have become what they are now—the most intensely cultivated and the most productive intellectual corporations the world has ever seen.

The student who repairs to them sees in the list of classes and of professors a fair picture of the world of knowledge. Whatever he needs to know there is some one ready to teach him, some one competent to discipline him in the way of learning; whatever his special bent, let him but be able and diligent, and in due time he shall find distinction and a career. Among his professors he sees men whose names are known and revered throughout the civilized world; and their living example infects him with a noble ambition and a love for the spirit of work.

The Germans dominate the intellectual world by virtue of the same simple secret as that which made Napoleon the master of old Europe. They have declared that careers shall be open to talents and every Bursch marches with a professor's gown in his knapsack. Let him become a great scholar, or a man of science, and ministers will compete for his services. In Germany, they do not leave the chance of his holding the office he would render illustrious to the mercies of a hot canvass and the final wisdom of a mob of country parsons.

Moral and social science—one of the greatest and most fruitful of our future classes, I hope—at present lacks only one thing in our programme, and that is a teacher. A considerable want, no doubt; but it must be recollected that it is much better to want a teacher than to want the desire to learn.

Further, we need what, for want of a better name, I must call Physical Geography. What I mean is that which the Germans call *"Erdkunde."* It is a description of the earth, of its place and relation to other bodies; of its general structure and of its great features—winds, tides, mountains, plains: of the chief forms of the vegetable and animal worlds, of the varieties of man. It is the peg upon which the greatest quantity of useful and entertaining scientific information can be suspended.[5]

Literature is not upon the college programme; but I hope some day to see it there. For literature is the greatest of all sources of refined pleasure, and one of the great uses of a liberal education is to enable us to enjoy that pleasure. There is scope enough for the purposes of liberal education in the study of the rich treasures of our own language alone. All that is needed is direction, and the cultivation of a refined taste by attention to sound criticism. But there is no reason why French and German should not be mastered sufficiently to read what is worth reading in those languages with pleasure and with profit.

And finally, by-and-by, we must have history; treated not as a succession of battles and dynasties; not as a series of biographies; not as evidence that Providence has always been on the side of either Whigs or Tories, but as the development of man in times past and in other conditions than our own.

FOOTNOTES:

[5] Professor Huxley's "Physiography," published by D. Appleton & Co., New York, is an excellent text-book for the study he here recommends. It has been drawn upon for two chapters of the first volume of "Masterpieces of Science." Equally to be recommended are "Physical Geography" and "Elementary Physical Geography," by Prof. W. M. Davis, of Harvard University, published by Ginn & Co., Boston.

SCIENCE AND CULTURE

PROFESSOR T. H. HUXLEY

[Sir Josiah Mason's Science College, Birmingham, was opened in 1880 with an address by Professor Huxley which appears in full in the third volume of his essays published by D. Appleton & Co., New York. As here given passages of local and temporary interest have been omitted.]

From the time that the first suggestion to introduce physical science into ordinary education was timidly whispered, until now, the advocates of scientific education have met with opposition of two kinds. On the one hand, they have been pooh-poohed by the men of business who pride themselves on being the representatives of practicality; while, on the other hand, they have been excommunicated by the classical scholars in their capacity of Levites in charge of the ark of culture and monopolists of liberal education.

The practical men believed that the idol whom they worship—rule of thumb—has been the source of the past prosperity and will suffice for the future welfare of the arts and manufactures. They were of opinion that science is speculative rubbish; that theory and practice have nothing to do with one another; and that the scientific habit of mind is an impediment, rather than an aid, in the conduct of ordinary affairs.

I have used the past tense in speaking of the practical men—for although they were very formidable thirty years ago, I am not sure that the pure species has not been extirpated. In fact, so far as mere argument goes, they have been subjected to such a fire from the netherworld that it is a miracle if any have escaped. But I have remarked that your typical practical man has an unexpected resemblance to one of Milton's angels. His spiritual wounds, such as are inflicted by logical weapons, may be as deep as a well and as wide as a church-door, but beyond shedding a few drops of ichor, celestial or otherwise, he is no whit the worse.

How often have we not been told that the study of physical science is incompetent to confer culture; that it touches none of the higher problems of life; and, what is worse, that the continual devotion to scientific studies tends to generate a narrow and bigoted belief in the applicability of scientific methods to the search after truth of all kinds? How frequently one has reason to observe that no reply to a troublesome argument tells so well as calling its author a "mere scientific specialist." And, as I am afraid it is not permissible to speak of this form of opposition to scientific education in the past tense; may we not expect to be told that this, not only omission, but prohibition, of "mere literary instruction and education" is a patent example of scientific narrow-mindedness?

I am not acquainted with Sir Josiah Mason's reasons for declaring that the college shall make no provision for "mere literary instruction and education," but if, as I apprehend the case, he refers to the ordinary classical course of our schools and universities by the name of "mere literary instruction and education," I venture to offer sundry reasons of my own in support of that action.

For I hold very strongly by two convictions. The first is, that neither the discipline nor the subject-matter of classical education is of such direct value to the student of physical science as to justify the expenditure of valuable time upon either; and the second is, that for the purpose of attaining real culture, an exclusively scientific education is at least as effectual as an exclusively literary education.

I need hardly point out to you that these opinions, especially the latter, are diametrically opposed to those of the great majority of educated

Englishmen, influenced as they are by school and university traditions. In their belief, culture is obtainable only by a liberal education; and a liberal education is synonymous, not merely with education and instruction in literature, but in one particular form of literature, namely, that of Greek and Roman antiquity. They hold that the man who has learned Latin and Greek, however little, is educated; while he who is versed in other branches of knowledge, however deeply, is a more or less respectable specialist, not admissible into the cultured caste. The stamp of the educated man, the university degree, is not for him.

I am too well acquainted with the generous catholicity of spirit, the true sympathy with scientific thought, which pervades the writings of our chief apostle of culture to identify him with these opinions; and yet one may cull from one and another of those epistles to the Philistines, which so much delight all who do not answer to that name, sentences which lend them some support.

Mr. Arnold tells us that the meaning of culture is "to know the best that has been thought and said in the world." It is the criticism of life contained in literature. That criticism regards "Europe as being, for intellectual and spiritual purposes, one great confederation, bound to a joint action and working to a common result; and whose members have, for their common outfit, a knowledge of Greek, Roman, and Eastern antiquity, and of one another. Special, local, and temporary advantages being put out of account, that modern nation will in the intellectual and spiritual sphere make most progress, which most thoroughly carries out this program. And what is that but saying that we too, all of us, as individuals, the more thoroughly we carry it out, shall make the more progress?"[6]

We have here to deal with two distinct propositions. The first, that a criticism of life is the essence of culture; the second, that literature contains the materials which suffice for the construction of such criticism.

I think that we must all assent to the first proposition. For culture certainly means something quite different from learning or technical skill. It implies the possession of an ideal, and the habit of critically estimating the value of things by comparison with a theoretic standard. Perfect culture should supply a complete theory of life, based upon a clear knowledge alike of its possibilities and of its limitations.

But we may agree to all this, and yet strongly dissent from the assumption that literature alone is competent to supply this knowledge. After having learnt all that Greek, Roman, and Eastern antiquity have thought and said, and all that modern literature have to tell us, it is not self-evident that we have laid a sufficiently broad and deep foundation for that criticism of life, which constitutes culture.

Indeed, to anyone acquainted with the scope of physical science, it is not at all evident. Considering progress only in the "intellectual and spiritual sphere," I find myself wholly unable to admit that either nations or individuals will really advance if their common outfit draws nothing from the stores of physical science. I should say that an army, without weapons of precision and with no particular base of operations, might more hopefully enter upon a campaign on the Rhine than a man, devoid of a knowledge of what physical science has done in the last century, upon a criticism of life.

The representatives of the Humanists, in the nineteenth century, take their stand upon classical education as the sole avenue to culture, as firmly as if we were still in the age of Renascence. Yet, surely, the present intellectual relations of the modern and the ancient worlds are profoundly different from those which obtained three centuries ago. Leaving aside the existence of a great and characteristically modern literature, of modern painting, and, especially, of modern music, there is one feature of the present state of the civilized world which separates it more widely from the Renascence, than the Renascence was separated from the middle ages.

This distinctive character of our own times lies in the vast and constantly increasing part which is played by natural knowledge. Not only is our daily life shaped by it, not only does the prosperity of millions of men depend upon it, but our whole theory of life has long been influenced, consciously or unconsciously, by the general conceptions of the universe, which have been forced upon us by physical science.

In fact, the most elementary acquaintance with the results of scientific investigation shows us that they offer a broad and striking contradiction to the opinion so implicitly credited and taught in the middle ages.

The notions of the beginning and the end of the world entertained by our forefathers are no longer credible. It is very certain that the earth is not the chief body in the material universe, and that the world is not subordinated to man's use. It is even more certain that nature is the expression of a definite order with which nothing interferes, and that the chief business of mankind is to learn that order and govern themselves accordingly. Moreover this scientific "criticism of life" presents itself to us with different credentials from any other. It appeals not to authority, nor to what anybody may have thought or said, but to nature. It admits that all our interpretations of natural fact are more or less imperfect and symbolic, and bids the learner seek for truth not among words but among things. It warns us that the assertion which outstrips evidence is not only a blunder but a crime.

The purely classical education advocated by the representatives of the Humanists in our day, gives no inkling of all this. A man may be a better scholar than Erasmus, and know no more of the chief causes of the present intellectual fermentation than Erasmus did. Scholarly and pious persons, worthy of all respect, favour us with allocutions upon the sadness of the antagonism of science to their mediæval way of thinking, which betray an ignorance of the first principles of scientific investigation, an incapacity for understanding what a man of science means by veracity, and an unconsciousness of the weight of established scientific truths, which is almost comical.

There is no great force in the *tu quoque* [thou too] argument, or else the advocates of scientific education might fairly enough retort upon the modern Humanists that they may be learned specialists, but that they possess no such sound foundation for a criticism of life as deserves the name of culture. And, indeed, if we were disposed to be cruel, we might urge that the Humanists have brought this reproach upon themselves, not because they are too full of the spirit of the ancient Greek, but because they lack it.

The period of the Renascence is commonly called that of the "Revival of Letters," as if the influences then brought to bear upon the mind of Western Europe had been wholly exhausted in the field of literature. I think it is very commonly forgotten that the revival of science, effected by the same agency, although less conspicuous, was not less momentous.

In fact, the few and scattered students of nature of that day picked up the clue to her secrets exactly as it fell from the hands of the Greeks a thousand years before. The foundations of mathematics were so well laid by them, that our children learn their geometry from a book written for the schools of Alexandria two thousand years ago. Modern astronomy is the natural continuation and development of the work of Hipparchus and of Ptolemy; modern physics of that of Democritus and of Archimedes. It was long before modern biological science outgrew the knowledge bequeathed to us by Aristotle, by Theophrastus, and by Galen.

We cannot know all the best thoughts and sayings of the Greeks unless we know what they thought about natural phenomena. We cannot fully apprehend their criticism of life unless we understand the extent to which that criticism was affected by scientific conceptions. We falsely pretend to be the inheritors of their culture, unless we are penetrated, as the best minds among them were, with an unhesitating faith that the free employment of reason, in accordance with scientific methods, is the sole method of reaching truth.

Thus I venture to think that the pretensions of our modern Humanists to the possession of the monopoly of culture and to the exclusive inheritance of the spirit of antiquity must be abated, if not abandoned. But I should be very sorry that anything I have said should be taken to imply a desire on my part to depreciate the value of classical education, as it might be and as it sometimes is. The native capacities of mankind vary no less than their opportunities; and while culture is one, the road by which one man may best reach it is widely different from that which is most advantageous to another. Again, while scientific education is yet inchoate and tentative,

classical education is thoroughly well organized upon the practical experience of generations of teachers.

I am the last person to question the importance of genuine literary education, or to suppose that intellectual culture can be complete without it. An exclusively scientific training will bring about a mental twist as surely as an exclusively literary training. The value of the cargo does not compensate for a ship's being out of trim; and I should be very sorry to think that the Scientific College would turn out none but lop-sided men.

There is no need, however, that such a catastrophe should happen. Instruction in English, French, and German is provided, and thus the three greatest literatures of the modern world are made accessible to the student.

French and German, and especially the latter language, are absolutely indispensable to those who desire full knowledge in any department of science. But even supposing that the knowledge of these languages acquired is not more than sufficient for purely scientific purposes, every Englishman has, in his native tongue, an almost perfect instrument of literary expression; and, in his own literature, models of every kind of literary excellence. If an Englishman cannot get literary culture out of his Bible, his Shakespeare, his Milton, neither, in my belief, will the profoundest study of Homer and Sophocles, Virgil and Horace, give it to him.

Thus, since the constitution of the College makes sufficient provision for literary as well as for scientific education, and since artistic instruction is also contemplated, it seems to me that a fairly complete culture is offered to all who are willing to take advantage of it.

But I am not sure that at this point the "practical" man, scotched but not slain, may ask what all this talk about culture has to do with an Institution, the object of which is defined to be "to promote the prosperity of the manufactures and the industry of the country." He may suggest that what is wanted for this end is not culture, nor even a purely scientific discipline, but simply a knowledge of applied science.

I often wish that this phrase, "applied science," had never been invented. For it suggests that there is a sort of scientific knowledge of direct practical use, which can be studied apart from another sort of scientific knowledge, which is of no practical utility, and which is termed "pure science." But there is no more complete fallacy than this. What people call applied science is nothing but the application of pure science to particular classes of problems. It consists of deductions from those general principles, established by reasoning and observation, which constitute pure science. No one can safely make these deductions until he has a firm grasp of the principles; and he can obtain that grasp only by personal experience of the operations of observation and of reasoning on which they are founded.

Almost all the processes employed in the arts and manufactures fall within the range either of physics or of chemistry. In order to improve them, one must thoroughly understand them; and no one has a chance of really understanding them, unless he has obtained that mastery of principles and that habit of dealing with facts, which is given by long-continued and well-directed purely scientific training in the physical and the chemical laboratory. So that there really is no question as to the necessity of purely scientific discipline, even if the work of the College were limited by the narrowest interpretation of its stated aims.

And, as to the desirableness of a wider culture than that yielded by science alone, it is to be recollected that the improvement of manufacturing processes is only one of the conditions which contribute to the prosperity of industry. Industry is a means and not an end; and mankind work only to get something which they want. What that something is depends partly on their innate, and partly on their acquired, desires.

If the wealth resulting from prosperous industry is to be spent upon the gratification of unworthy desires, if the increasing perfection of manufacturing processes is to be accompanied by an increasing debasement of those who carry them on, I do not see the good of industry and prosperity.

Now it is perfectly true that men's views of what is desirable depend upon their characters; and that the innate proclivities to which we give that name are not touched by any amount of instruction. But it does not follow that even mere intellectual education may not, to an indefinite extent, modify the practical manifestation of the characters of men in their actions, by supplying them with motives unknown to the ignorant. A pleasure-loving character will have pleasure of some sort; but, if you give him the choice, he may prefer pleasures which do not degrade him to those which do. And this choice is offered to every man, who possesses in literary or artistic culture a never-failing source of pleasures, which are neither withered by age, nor staled by custom, nor embittered in the recollection by the pangs of self-reproach.

If the Institution opened to-day fulfils the intention of its founder, the picked intelligences among all classes of the population of this district will pass through it. No child born in Birmingham, henceforward, if he have the capacity to profit by the opportunities offered to him, first in the primary and other schools, and afterwards in the Scientific College, need fail to obtain, not merely the instruction, but the culture most appropriate to the conditions of his life.

Within these walls, the future employer and the future artisan may sojourn together for a while, and carry, through all their lives, the stamp of the influences then brought to bear upon them. Hence, it is not beside the mark to remind you that the prosperity of industry depends not merely upon the improvement of manufacturing processes, not merely upon the ennobling of the individual character, but upon a third condition, namely, a clear understanding of the conditions of social life, on the part of both the capitalist and the operative, and their agreement upon common principles of social action. They must learn that social phenomena are as much the expression of natural laws as any others; that no social arrangements can be permanent unless they harmonize with the requirements of social statics and dynamics; and that, in the nature of things, there is an arbiter whose decisions execute themselves.

But this knowledge is only to be obtained by the application of the methods of investigation adopted in physical researches to the investigation of the phenomena of society. Hence, I confess, I should like to see one addition made to the excellent scheme of education propounded for the College, in the shape of provision for the teaching of Sociology. For though we are all agreed that party politics are to have no place in the instruction of the College; yet in this country, practically governed as it is now by universal suffrage, every man who does his duty must exercise political functions. And, if the evils which are inseparable from the good of political liberty are to be checked, if the perpetual oscillation of nations between anarchy and despotism is to be replaced by the steady march of self-restraining freedom; it will be because men will gradually bring themselves to deal with political, as they now deal with scientific questions; to be as ashamed of undue haste and partisan prejudice in the one case as the other; and to believe that the machinery of society is at least as delicate as that of a spinning jenny, and as little likely to be improved by the meddling of those who have not taken the trouble to master the principles of its action.

www.ingramcontent.com/pod-product-compliance
Lightning Source LLC
Chambersburg PA
CBHW081117080526
44587CB00021B/3639